IN RUIN RECONCILED

JOAN DE VERE

"IN RUIN RECONCILED"

A Memoir of Anglo-Ireland
1913 – 1959

WITH A FOREWORD BY MARY LELAND

THE LILLIPUT PRESS
1990

First published in 1990 by
THE LILLIPUT PRESS LTD
4 Rosemount Terrace, Arbour Hill,
Dublin 7, Ireland.

A CIP record for this
title is available from
The British Library.

ISBN 0 946640 43 2

Jacket design by Jole Bortoli
Set in 11 on 13 Bembo by
Seton Music Graphics Ltd of Bantry
and printed in England by
Billings & Sons Ltd of Worcester

I heard a woman's voice that wailed
   Between the sandhills and the sea:
The famished sea-bird past me sailed
   Into the dim infinity.

I stood on boundless, rainy moors:
   Far off I saw a great Rock loom;
The grey dawn smote its iron doors;
   And then I knew it was a Tomb.

Two queenly shapes before the grate
   Watched, couchant on the barren ground;
Two regal shapes in ruined state,
   One Gael, one Norman; both discrowned.

(Aubrey de Vere, 'In Ruin Reconciled')

CONTENTS

LIST OF ILLUSTRATIONS

PUBLISHER'S NOTE AND ACKNOWLEDGMENTS

Joan Wynne-Jones, *née* de Vere, died on the 17th of September 1989, after completion of the manuscript but in the knowledge of its impending publication. The publisher would especially like to thank the following for their help in final preparation of both manuscript and proofs: Margaret Burns, Brian Fitzelle, Mary Leland, Angela Rohan, and Grace, Martin and Patrick Wynne-Jones.

FOREWORD

There is a photograph of Joan de Vere, taken when she was about twenty-one, full face. It is beautiful; she was a very beautiful girl. But it is also open, expectant, and now it stands among family snaps, postcards, the coloured litter of the last years of her life, its black and white still glowing with the radiance of her optimism.

Optimism is a kind of courage, when all is said and done. To be able to expect the best – that suggests a faith in humankind which surely, in a lifetime, must at some point have been threatened to its foundations. In Joan that faith often wore the face of expectation: she believed in good, she expected goodness. For anyone less confident of responsive generosity, meeting her, coming to terms with her acceptance of one's own, perhaps dilatory, best intentions, could be disconcerting.

We met through a professional kinship. Some personal adjustments had to be made – I hope on both sides. Wynne, her husband (Martin, that is, but Wynne to the family), seemed to laugh at hearing some of our careful exchanges. Once or twice it was even possible to suspect that he was enjoying himself as a referee – utterly impartial, but keeping the score with some relish.

It would not be true to say that we collaborated. Joan needed some help – but much less than she thought she needed. She was writing this book and, having begun, discovered that her technical skill could not quite keep pace with her creative memory. And pace meant time for her. She had been ill; she had come to recognize time as a force in itself, something unpredictable, to be managed, to be anticipated at least, if not at the last outwitted.

All that was required was the organization of chapters and even that she could quickly do herself, once she knew what was wanted. What was not quite so easy was what was not, perhaps, so necessary – some editorial acknowledgment that the reader might not move as quickly through this flood of life as Joan herself could do. Her own certainties, her own sense of direction, needed no supporting structures. It took her just a little while to get used to the idea that she might encourage potential readers towards the truths of her story rather than just state the facts as facts, logical and surely perfectly obvious.

But some things were not obvious. There were mysteries in her own life. The dilemma was how to reconcile a profound sense of herself as a private person with her desire now to reveal her life to others. Perhaps she thought that she could reveal the facts, the observations, the fun, the accomplishments, everything which was true, without revealing the most essential truths, without being revelatory even to herself?

In writing this book, therefore, she must have had to ask many questions of herself. It was no longer enough to know; now she had to explain. One way out was to insist that this book is not about her, as a person, or even fully about her life. The origin of the desire to write it was, I think, her awareness that she had been born into, and had lived for many years in, a world which was then entering eclipse. But Joan had already written her biography of the Big House in her life, *The Abiding Enchantment of Curragh Chase* (Cló Duanaire); for its purposes she had researched her antecedents, had come to know them while they stood in the full sunlight of their ancestral certainties.

Although the details of her birth and parentage must have been well known to the important people in her life, Joan herself never learned them – except that her birthday was the 11th of January 1913. She did discover that her parents had been friends of her adoptive mother, and in some way connected with the bishop's palace at Bishop Auckland in Co. Durham. It was from there that she was adopted, by Isabel, daughter of Bishop Moule of Durham, and her husband, Robert Stephen Vere de Vere, Ll.B.(Cantab.), B.L., of Curragh Chase in Co. Limerick. They were childless; Isabel desperately wanted a child – and it was acceptable for the landed gentry to adopt a girl provided the estate was entailed. Curragh Chase was.

Like Vita Sackville-West at Knole, Joan fell hopelessly in love with Curragh Chase. (And like Vita, who, according to Virginia Woolf's fantasy in a letter to Jacques Raverat, kept all her ancestors 'stretched in coffins . . . under her dining-room floor', Joan slept as a child in a room next door to which a coffin containing a child's skeleton had once been found under the floorboards.) It gave her a playground of 800 acres of woodland and pasture, farmyard and dairy, kitchen garden, pleasure-grounds, lake and stream, deer park and lime avenue.

There was a Big House, there still is: a composed grey skeleton, roofless. Its state today is not the result of violent politics – a proposed IRA reprisal burning in the War of Independence was cancelled because of the de Veres' status and good reputation as landlords in the area – or of abandonment (although Sir Stephen, in the end, did leave it, retiring to Cyprus) or neglect. It perished in an accidental fire in 1941, at Christmas-time, when there was no help about, no telephone; the water pressure was low and the fire brigade late. And although for years afterwards Joan and her family returned to visit Curragh Chase, where her mother continued to live in an estate cottage, this was the termination of a fundamental relationship which had sustained, perhaps even created, Joan as the imaginative observer of animal as well as human life.

She did not have a very happy childhood, although it must have seemed a privileged one. She grew up in a time when even the most wanted children were left to the care of nannies and governesses – and her father's career in the colonial service took her parents away from home for long periods of her youth. She was solitary, xiv and became self-reliant, if not self-sufficient. And then she was caught in that extraordinary trap laid by custom for the well-bred young woman of those days. Having been forced, all her young life, to practise independence, judgment and self-control, she was forbidden to exercise any of these qualities when the time came for the major decisions about her future life.

She wanted to train for a profession; that could not be allowed. She wanted to marry a certain man; that could not be allowed. She did not want to live in the colonies with her parents and arrange flowers and play tennis — that was to be her life.

Her way out of this dilemma is part of the story of this book: she tells it as it happened. But she could not assess it as others could who saw it or who shared it with her. In 1936 she married a man who was then a Director of Education in Grenada. On his return to Ireland he became a teacher and later a clergyman of the Church of Ireland, and for nearly twenty years they worked together in the parishes of Ballyorgan and Knockaney in Co. Limerick, in the diocese of Cashel. They had five children; one, Patrick, was born at Curragh Chase in the Octagon Room.

She immensely enjoyed all of this. She was a terrific parish worker and Secretary for the British Legion in Co. Limerick. There were nineteen acres at Knockaney, where she bred dogs and fowl and minded the trees in the spinney beyond the garden. She gave her children a happy childhood, helping them to be confident, as well as independent.

Joan had a nature ready for enthusiasm, poised for rapture. It was this rapturous response which she poured into her love for Curragh Chase. As that matured, and she came to understand the frailty of these old great houses, she understood also how faint and faraway to many must seem the life they once contained. It was not that she mourned that life, although she did mourn Curragh Chase; it was that she appreciated it.

The house in its history is typical of that other Irishness we still seem to find it hard to accommodate: that Irishness which stands gutted and forlorn, its lead and gutters sold or stolen, its windows blind, its gardens overgrown, its timber felled. '*Cad a dhéanfaimid feasta gan adhmad?*'

We don't know how to respond to that pile of history: look at Bowenscourt, look at Woodhill House, Look – and again one looks in vain – at Drogheda Grammar School, where Wynne once taught.

But Joan appreciated also the life she grasped with both hands and all her heart when she agreed to marry Martin Wynne Jones. When Wynne retired they went to live in Buttevant, near Kilcolman, Spenser's castle. By now a devoted naturalist, Joan began to write for several newspapers and magazines, but it was not until they moved to Cork and their home among the trees on the College Road that she felt able to move into other subjects, writing book reviews and then, at last, settling to the only expression she could now give to her passion for Curragh Chase.

The estate had been sold to the Forestry and Land Commission – which quickly put an end to the lime avenue and engaged in what Joan describes here as 'wholesale' tree-cutting. At least she lived to see this amazing policy reversed and to partake in the public enjoyment of the lands she had loved so dearly. She had never feared its ghosts, she had relished its legends, and she has now written its chronicles. From now on those of us who walk beneath the trees of Curragh Chase, who stand at the headstones for Ranger the red setter, or Hadji the Persian cat, and feel some curiosity about the people who made this place, can know that their history has been told and that, like the old estate itself, it is available to anyone who cares to seek it out.

Did the Castle baby, the young woman with that open, joyous face, get what she hoped for out of life? I believe she did. Her marriage, certainly, was joyous, and she was happily proud of her children for themselves. And who would have wanted to disappoint her? I met her only at the end of her life, but even then there was that expression of bright, unfearful hopefulness.

Mary Leland
Cork, January 1990

1.   A portrait of the author as a young woman in the early 1930s

2. Sir Stephen de Vere (the poet's brother), Bishop Butler and
   Lord Emly, during the mid nineteenth century

3. The long east front of Curragh Chase, seen from across the lake

4. Mrs Isabel de Vere, the author's mother

5. Joan de Vere and her husband Martin Wynne-Jones

6. Joan de Vere with her lemur and parents in front of their house in the Seychelle Islands

7. Eamon de Valera and his daughter Máirín, guests of Isabel de Vere at Curragh Chase on 13 December 1955

8. The south façade of Curragh Chase in 1956, prior to its sale to the Forestry Commission

IN RUIN RECONCILED

ONE

Beginnings

ONLY RECENTLY has it been fully understood what an immense effect the experiences of the early years have on the emotional development of a personality.

Auckland Castle, seat of the Bishop of Durham, at Bishop Auckland, County Durham, which stretched in all directions with confident abandon, was the background of some of my first memories. Born on the 11th of January 1913, I was known as the 'Castle baby' until I was adopted by Stephen de Vere and his wife Isabel, *née* Moule, daughter of Bishop Handley Moule. My pram would be placed outside the back door where the metallic clatter of cutlery being cleaned and sorted in the butler's pantry could be clearly heard. As I grew older I got to know every corner of the massive building. At three or four years of age I would stand in the middle of the great state room with the portraits of bishops looking down upon me and attend morning prayers in the private chapel in which the entire adult household would gather, and where I was the only child.

My nursery was one of the rooms in a long passage called 'Scotland' because it pointed in that direction. When in the dark I awoke tearful from nightmares or secret fears, it seemed miles from the warm heart of the house.

Worse still, the lavatory was two flights of stairs and several landings away so that sometimes disaster overtook the small person before she could get there.

I was a solemn and thoughtful child already learning to compensate for my lack of companionship by retreating into that world of make-believe and fantasy which was to make periods of solitude necessary to me for the rest of my life. I believe I was an engaging little figure with a round face and fringed hair. In summer girls of that period wore 'for best' starched frocks embroidered at the hem, often with a sash at the waist, and starched hats of the same material encircled with a ribbon. During winter we wore serge skirts and jerseys, with velvet frocks for parties, and an outing involved putting on gaiters with their seemingly endless series of buttons.

It was a time when 'elders and betters' were the first to be considered. Among the upper classes, children, until they reached years of discretion, were sometimes loved, often only tolerated, but practically always kept out of sight and sound. Along the vast passages of the Castle I wandered with my nursemaid, lost in my own dimension of existence, brushing against the adult world, treading the carefully laid paths of everyday life while not far off, across the sea, hundreds of young men were dying every day. In the streets of our own town black became more and more the garb of the womenfolk.

I had several changes of nursemaids, but most were kind enough and would share with me the strictly rationed sweets they bought, lick for lick. My adoptive mother looked after me on the girls' afternoon off. I was a child thirsty for affection, of which there was not a great deal at that stage of my life.

Discipline was rigorous and instant obedience insisted upon. On one occasion this system rather rebounded on itself. My mother had an interesting and unusual phobia which amounted to a paralysing horror of feathers. There was a large gathering in the drawing-room of all the clergy wives of the diocese. I had been playing in the garden wearing a Red Indian feather head-dress and as I came through the front door she called me somewhat peremptorily. Knowing her likely reaction I tried to make excuses, but was once more summoned to come at once. As I entered the crowded room my mother backed away in fear and hid herself behind one of the large curtains.

Mealtimes were often bleak. Children's preferences in food were seldom considered seriously and it was believed to be excellent training to insist that every morsel on the plate should be finished up, which in my case often led to pieces of congealed fat being solemnly placed before me, meal after meal, until consumed. If one raised any objection one was confronted with the remark, 'How many starving children in Africa would be glad of it!' Unfortunately, at that age one did not have the courage to retort, 'Why not send it to them?'

Food at the Castle was adequate but plain and strictly rationed for all alike. A little butter was allowed for the old and very young, such as my grandfather and myself. However, when he heard that the servants were turning up their noses at the ubiquitous margarine, he refused to have any butter at all in the house.

Halfway up the back stairs of the Castle was a small room known as the 'housekeeper's room', although at that period no housekeeper was employed. Here I had my unsupervised breakfast, usually a boiled egg which would normally have been considered a treat in those years of shortages, but I hated eggs and they did not agree with me. Although I sometimes ate the yolk I invariably threw the white behind the long case-clock in the corner of the room. When spring-cleaning time came round the smelly pile was discovered but the kind-hearted staff kept my secret and smiled at my resourcefulness.

The household staff was headed by Ernest Alexander, the butler, who lived in his own married quarters. He had served many bishops and was to serve several others afterwards. I always treated him with great respect and addressed him as Mr Alexander. There was the footman with a harelip and cleft palate, which for some reason exempted him from war service (only the best and healthiest were sent out to die). A typical blowzy cook presided over the huge range in the large solidly built kitchen. Then there were two maids in blue print dresses, large white aprons and caps. The chauffeur, Hubbins, lived outside with his family in his own cottage.

Being so young, the impact of sadness brought by a disastrous war touched me very little and in the quiet of the bishop's palace life went on much as usual. There was, however, one occasion when the reality of the hostilities came very close.

At one period, as is well recorded, the Germans employed large airships (or Zeppelins) to seek out and attack suitable targets. The north of England, being largely an industrial area, was picked out for more than one of these raids. They were looking for certain large buildings used as munition factories or other places useful for the war effort. One such raid took place in 1917. The target sought was Newcastle but the strong winds blew the cumbersome dirigible off course, and it found itself over Bishop Auckland.

Those were the years of my nightmare-ridden occupancy of the remote nursery. The gas light was always left on slightly in my room to allay my fears but actually it only cast strange and fearsome shadows in the corners. On this occasion it began to dip up and down. I now know that this was a prearranged warning signal before, in the interest of the 'black-out', it went out altogether. A strange humming sound pervaded everything and from time to time a light shone directly into my window. These gas-filled cylinders had no searchlights as we now understand them, and in order to reconnoitre let down a form of cage to a dangerously low level for the 'spotter', or man inside who manipulated the searchlight.

At this moment Ernest Alexander arrived, hastily bundled me in a blanket, and ran with me a considerable distance to the large semi-basement stone-flagged hall. Here the entire household finally gathered except for my grandfather, who was away at the time on a pastoral visit to a distant part of his diocese. I can still smell the damp earth beneath those stone flags on which we huddled in trepidation. Finally the humming stopped and the fragile monster and its crew moved elsewhere, only to be brought down in flames not far off.

Although they were our enemies, most people felt an unwilling admiration for these brave men. Their aircraft was extremely vulnerable and few returned safely to base, and yet on this occasion they were prepared to expose themselves to danger in order to discover whether

Auckland Castle was the correct target. This type of warfare did not continue for long as Zeppelins were found to be too easily shot down.

Because of the Zeppelin alarms it was decided to send me away for some weeks to a small country rectory in a village on the border of counties Durham and Yorkshire. It was a bleak but friendly place, a bare stone building near the churchyard which I feel must have resembled Haworth Parsonage where the Brontës lived. There I joined a family of three children and we played in the open countryside.

Among the stretches of moorland and heather, grouse chicks were so plentiful in the late spring that it was easily possible to catch one or two by hand. The sturdy farming folk, largely self-supporting and untouched by rationing, would occasionally kill a pig and distribute portions among the neighbours. The village shop had few luxuries and sweets were practically unobtainable but I remember it was sometimes possible to get lumps of home-made chocolate; this was not very sweet and appeared to consist of cocoa with a binding ingredient, but it was definitely better than nothing.

When it became obvious that the air raids had ceased I returned to live in the Castle, leaving it occasionally to spend periods in the local vicarage. The vicar, Lord Thurlow, then one of the few peers to be ordained, had four children, all boys. The twins were about my own age, and I spent many weeks sharing the warm, friendly nursery with them. There was a lot to be said for the nursery world of those days. Nanny was infinitely firm, infinitely kind, and infinitely wise. Dressed when indoors in voluminous print frock and apron, and when outside in flowing veil and blue uniform coat, she was the queen of our small world.

Stretching for several miles away from the Castle was a beautiful park open to the public. Part of it was bordered by horse-chestnut trees, pink and white varieties alternating, and in early summer their lovely flowers stretched like candles towards the heavens. Farther on, ancient pit ponies who had served much of their vigorous life in darkness underground lived out a peaceful retirement in the paddocks. Elsewhere an impressively structured deer house now served as a winter shelter for sheep, as deer were no longer kept.

Along the tortuous stretches of this park every fine afternoon Nanny would take the young Thurlows and myself for a walk while a nursemaid pushed the youngest member of the family in a large blue pram. We then returned to nursery tea. Golden syrup was a great treat in those years of shortages, but somehow a tin was usually on the tea-table and the most effective punishment meted out for misbehaviour was to deny us this delicacy on our bread. If the day was wet there were plenty of toys to amuse us at home and a large dappled rocking-horse, the size of a real pony, dominated the nursery.

My grandfather, Handley Carr Glynn Moule, was a delightful person of great spirituality. He was a convinced evangelical and his moral code would today be considered too strict. He was a strong Sabbatarian and would remonstrate with groups of miners if he found them playing football in the park on a Sunday. Bishops had a much easier life then than now. My grandfather had a chauffeur and two chaplains, one resident and one visiting. It is no wonder that he had time to write a number of devotional books which were widely read at the time.

He was always kind to me and I have very happy memories of him. When he was away for a period he would write me little rhymes:

> My darling Joan, thou child so grand,
> The dear card, written by thy hand,
> Has to thy Grandad given a pleasure
> So great it is quite hard to measure.
>
> You ask me if I'm well, I AM!
> I'm getting on quite well, dear lamb,
> But oh! how glad I shall be when
> I see my little Joan again.

Grandfather was the son of a country vicar who had served for over fifty years in the parish of Fordington in Dorsetshire. He was one of a large family of sons and, in order to supplement his meagre income, his father took in other boys to educate with his own family. Handley's own scholarly achievements earned him a place at Cambridge University where he received several special awards. Later he became Principal of Ridley Hall Theological Training College, from where he was transferred to be the bishop of the diocese of Durham and was one of two bishops who officiated at the coronations of Edward VII and George V. All the Moule brothers did well, two others becoming bishops in the mission field.

Their father was also a strict evangelical. His unbending attitude on moral issues made him unpopular at first, but when an epidemic swept through the village he nursed the sick in person and fearlessly attacked the government for its lack of attention to hygiene in these remote parts. His stand on the villagers' behalf earned him and his family esteem and affection in the locality.

Growing up not far away was a young boy of about the same age as the Moule brothers called Thomas Hardy, later to become known as the 'Bard of Dorset'. He came from a relatively poor background and the Reverend Moule, recognizing his talents, befriended him and helped him in his education. The Moule brothers were gifted artists, as was Hardy himself, and they all used to go sketching together. I have in my possession some exquisite watercolours by Henry Moule, the eldest of the brothers, portraying country scenes near Fordington, much of which is now engulfed by suburbia. His painting of Hardy's cottage is used on the jacket of the biography *Young Thomas Hardy* by Robert Gittings.

Handley married Mary Elliott, my grandmother, who was made of rather sterner stuff but who had a very warm heart. She would stand with me in a passage half-way up the front stairs where there was a large cuckoo clock, contriving to make the bird come out and give tongue continually for my amusement. They had two daughters, Tessie, who died of tuberculosis in her late teens, and Isabel Catherine, my mother.

Isabel, who was to dedicate her life to helping the poor and the underprivileged, was unusually beautiful as a girl, and also inherited the brains of the family. In 1906 she married an Irishman, R.S.V. de Vere. These were my adoptive parents.

My father's name had originally been Vere O'Brien, of the Inchiquin family, but when he inherited his County Limerick estate, Curragh Chase, through the female line, it was on condition that he assume the surname of the family which had lived there for generations. He therefore became Robert Stephen Vere de Vere. The poet Tennyson, author of the poem 'Lady Clara Vere de Vere',* who was a friend of the de Veres, stayed at Curragh Chase for five weeks in 1848. When my father's great-uncle Aubrey, the well-known poet, asked him why he had so used their name, Tennyson replied, 'Because I liked it.' At Cambridge my father was so ribbed that he dropped the first portion and became 'de Vere' only.

Like my mother, he had lost his sister at an early age and was the only child remaining to the family. When he left university my father qualified as a barrister at the Inner Temple and then practised his legal calling in the Colonial Service in such exotic locations as the New Hebrides, the Seychelles, Cyprus, and Grenada in the West Indies where he was Chief Justice. He returned to Curragh Chase after each posting, and it was there that I was brought at the end of the First World War.

*Containing the celebrated lines,
    'Kind hearts are more than coronets,
    And simple faith than Norman blood.'

TWO

Elders and Betters:
A Solitary Childhood

CURRAGH CHASE, near Adare in County Limerick, was a large estate of which my father was extremely fond and proud. He had a strong sense of position and family, and it was a grief to him that he had no son to inherit the property. Service abroad meant that he was unable to spend long periods in Ireland, but he would always return on leave with great happiness although I feel he would never have found fulfilment in life as a country gentleman.

The house looked east over a reed-fringed lake dotted with water-lilies and grounds which contained woods stretching to the distant Galtee mountains. It was built on land granted in about 1657 to Vere Hunt, a Royalist turned Cromwellian after the defeat at Naseby; his grandmother Jane Vere was a daughter of Aubrey de Vere, second son of the 15th Earl of Oxford, a line which later died out. For this reason the name Vere became attached to that of Hunt.

Much has been said about Irish landlords and their lack of care for tenants and evictions, and there were many of this kind, especially those who were absentee. But there were also good and caring landlords who iden-tified with those amongst whom they lived. The first Sir Vere Hunt married a daughter of the Bishop of Limerick in 1784 and lived at Curragh Chase into the early nineteenth century. He was a roistering, devil-may-care individual, who nonetheless concerned himself with the welfare of the poor and left interesting diaries that reflect the spirit of the times. (These were fortunately put aside for safe keeping by my mother at the suggestion of Robert Wyse Jackson, Bishop of Limerick.) In them he draws attention to workhouse and prison conditions and describes bringing them to the notice of appropriate authorities.

A charming story describes his passing through a certain town at the time of a murder trial. Entering the court, he discovered the accused to be a young man charged with killing someone in a faction fight. The judge appeared hesitant to pass sentence of death on one so young and remarked, 'Is there anyone in court who could speak as to your character?', to which the young man replied, 'There is no one here, my lord, that I know.' Sir Vere pushed himself forward in the courtroom and shouted out, 'You are a queer boy that don't know a friend when you see one.' Quick on the uptake, the youth said, ''Tis myself that is proud to see your honour here this day.' The judge remarked, 'Since you know this boy, will you tell us what you know of him?' 'I will, my lord,' replied Sir Vere, 'and what I can tell you is this — that from the very first day that I ever saw him until this minute, I never knew anything about him that was not very good.' The boy was released.

With Sir Aubrey de Vere, 2nd Baronet (1788 – 1846), the family dropped the Hunt by royal licence in 1832 and became de Vere only. They adopted the proud motto *Nihil vero verius*, 'nothing truer than truth', which my father in his time thought most suitable for a judge. Sir Aubrey was educated at Harrow with Byron and Peel and became an enlightened landlord who landscaped his estate and wrote a number of verse dramas such as the posthumously published *Mary Tudor,* as well as Wordsworthian sonnets about Ireland. His eldest son, Sir Vere Edmond de Vere, was musically inclined and died childless in 1880, when the second son, Stephen Edward (1812 – 1904), succeeded to the title and estate.

The best-known member of the family was Sir Aubrey's third son, Aubrey Thomas de Vere the poet (1814 – 1902), who went to Trinity College, Dublin, and belonged to a literary circle which included Tennyson, Carlyle, Wordsworth and Cardinal Newman. Aubrey became a Roman Catholic under the influence of Newman in 1851 and devoted much of his poetry to religious subjects.

Some consider that the second son is the most worthy of remembrance. Sir Stephen Edward de Vere was both

MP for Limerick from 1854 to 1859 and High Sheriff of the county in 1870, and took his duties most seriously. Becoming aware of the disgraceful conditions in the 'coffin ships' in which emigrants were being transported to Canada and America, in 1847 he booked a steerage passage to Quebec disguised in well-worn clothes. He was reputed to have been put in irons by the captain during the long sea journey. On his return he reported his findings to the House of Lords and, under the auspices of Earl Grey, improving legislation was put in hand.

Sir Stephen's literary attainments included translations from Horace. He had converted to Catholicism during his time in Canada and during his latter years lived on the island of Monare off Foynes in the Shannon estuary, and then in a two-roomed labourer's cottage, returning to Curragh Chase periodically to collect rents and settle accounts.

On Sir Stephen's death the baronetcy became extinct as there was no direct male heir. His younger brother Horace (Francis Horatio de Vere), the fifth son, a soldier who had been killed in battle, had three daughters. Curragh Chase therefore went to a nephew, son of Sir Stephen's sister, Elinor. He was my paternal grandfather, Aubrey Stephen O'Brien.

My father was in many ways typical of his class: upright, responsible, polite and gentlemanly to all, provided they kept to their appointed place. He enjoyed my companionship on walks around the estate, on which my mother seldom joined him. Our relationship was one of fondness rather than warmth. His mother, Lucy de Vere, was what the French call a *femme de tête*, a strong-minded woman. She had charge of Curragh Chase until her son came of age.

I spent part of my childhood with Granny during periods when my parents did not take me with them on postings abroad, and quickly learned she was a lady of strong views. My father must have temporarily forgotten or chosen to ignore this fact when, years before, he and a friend selected new wallpaper for a room in Curragh Chase. As soon as the old lady returned she tore down the new wallpaper. She was an astute business-woman who made the place pay, whereas my father geared himself towards qualifying as a barrister and later as a judge, and had little real knowledge of farming, depending upon a land agent and steward and money made abroad.

My mother, Isabel, had the greatest influence on my upbringing, but I shared the interests of my father and from an early age accompanied him as, slasher in hand, he tended to the young plantations. He was constantly occupied with thinning them or opening up vistas and walks. I learned from him to distinguish between beech and hornbeam, and to recognize the many forms of conifer through their diversity of cones.

It was on my lonely wanderings that I developed the love of nature which was to last me all my life. I felt a kinship with the smaller things of the forest and fields, the fungi and ferns growing in the dense woodland, the innumerable insects and creatures such as squirrels, hedgehogs and shrews, not to mention that world of the lake, where in the high trees of the island herons reared their gibbering young and a pair of dignified swans nested at the water's edge, while otters patrolled in search of perch. In the lake itself and the stream feeding it were caddis-worms, freshwater mussels to be searched for pearls and great pike constantly on the prowl, while on the surface floated a canopy of water-lilies.

There was a strong aspect of faerie in that tranquil place. It looked out towards Knock Feárna, the fairy mountain, and who could say whether some of 'the little people' were not resident with us also in that rocky cairn or hollow oak tree? Certainly, I was once led astray by these invisible midgets when, with a companion, I scoffed at the very idea of them from inside a grassy fairy ring. It took us ages to get home!

Shades of time past and people of another age lingered on in the grounds at Curragh Chase, but I was too young to be worried by them. It seemed to be quite natural that I should meet a couple in green livery and housemaid's apron and cap walking along the now over-grown 'servants' walk', or an old woman gathering sticks in front of a ruined cottage who curtsied to me and then vanished before my eyes. Others were less phlegmatic and would not venture along the wooded paths of the pleasure-ground after sunset.

Inside the house itself little had been changed and the many unique period pieces bought by previous genera-tions were left undisturbed in the quiet rooms where they had remained for many years. Some are worth enumerating: in the great hall, with its parquet floor composed of many coloured woods from the trees on the estate, was a frieze by Flaxman and a bust of Cardinal J. H. Newman. Beyond, in the saloon, was a towering plaster-cast (one of two known) of Michelangelo's *Moses* carrying Tablets of the Law, brought from Rome; here too was an enormous polar-bear skin and a buhl cabinet flanked by two huge pot-pourri-filled Ming vases, spoils from the Sack of Peking. A small display cabinet held the playing cards, stamps and money issued by the old Sir Vere Hunt when he owned Lundy Island in the Bristol Channel, and another contained a cross said to have been worn by King Charles I on the scaffold. The one painting in the house said to be of value was a portrait of the sculptor Roubiliac supposedly by William Hogarth. In the library the collection of leather-bound books consisted mainly of the Greek and Roman classics, while others such as the three pre-Famine volumes of wild flowers painted by Lucy Standish, wife to Sir Vere Edmond de Vere, eldest brother of Aubrey, reflected more local interests.

A gently curving staircase led upstairs to the two bedroom wings of the house. Just before the stairs curved to the left was a life-sized charcoal outline of Beatrice, drawn by the artist G. F. Watts while visiting the house. Beside Beatrice, Dante had also been portrayed, until a new and over-zealous employee was one day found vigorously removing all traces of it from the wall with a scrubbing-brush!

I learned not to impinge too much on the life-style of the adult world upstairs. There was no equality of status between children and their 'elders and betters', and definite respect was called for. It was behind the baize door which cut off the nursery and basement from the 'superior beings' on the other side that I felt most at home. The nursery and schoolroom were situated in the most extraordinary position at the very top of the back stairs with a clean drop on the other side of the banisters down to the stone flags below. Generations of children had called the schoolroom 'paradise on the back stairs' as it was a sure if humble retreat from the grown-up world.

In the cupboard were toys and books of varying age left by previous occupants. Among these were battered toy soldiers, heroes of many a battle; a zither; odd tiddly-winks and pieces of jigsaw and various Victorian children's books of nauseating sentimentality. There were two lovely dolls called Gracie and Rosie. They had long real hair and it was possible to curl it or plait it or arrange it in a number of ways. There was also a delightful baby doll. These three dolls were made of Parian chinaware from Germany. Their striking blue eyes were made on the same principle as the glass paperweights which are so much sought after today. In the reign of Queen Victoria most dolls, for the British market at any rate, had blue eyes. Queen Victoria was in no sense a thing of beauty but her eyes were her good point. Each doll had an elaborate outfit. The baby had flannel binders and long petticoats, as well as the beautifully embroidered long robes worn by infants at that period. The only items not included were nappies. The Victorians probably chose to ignore that most essential infant requisite. The older dolls had hand-stitched underwear including long frilly drawers, and the dresses were smocked or tucked.

In a corner of the room was a battered dolls' house with miniatures of the heavy ornate furniture of the period and a great assortment of dummy plaster edibles on colourful dishes. In the centre of the room was a round table of no particular value which had seen itself put to many uses. In winter a warm fire glowed in the grate making this small room one of the cosiest in the house. In a previous generation, old Sir Vere turned the children out of this room once a month and sat there to receive the tenants who came to pay their rents. One could picture them climbing the back stairs in none too content a humour. In our time the question of rent collections was a thing of the past as the tenants had become land-owners. Children were also thin on the ground but they alone made use of the room which, due to its previous association with accounts, was still often called 'the study'.

The great basement kitchen was my favourite place. When my parents were absent I would be left in the charge of Mrs Egglestone, or 'Eggie' as I called her, the cook-housekeeper. Her daughter, Jenny, was near my own age and, seated on the inglenook of the kitchen window, we would play with our dolls, give a hand with the wooden churn until the 'slap slap' of the forming butter could be heard, or go to the ice-cold dairy to watch the cream being skimmed from the large round pans of milk.

In the main part of the stately building, as one wandered through the vast hall, large saloon or book-lined library on a winter's evening, shadows leapt at one from every corner and the solitary flame of a candle did little to hasten their retreat. There was always a presence behind one, not malignant but persistent.

After I left the nursery, I was put to sleep in a large room at the top of the house known as the Green Room. It was well known that this room was haunted but it was felt that a child sleeping there would have a calming effect. Almost every night I would be kept awake by continual and peremptory knocking at the door which ceased only when I sat up in bed saying 'Come in'.

Nobody ever did. Sometimes there were mournful groans and sighs coming from behind a cupboard. In the dressing-room attached to the Green Room, a coffin had been discovered during renovations some sixty years previously. In it was the skeleton of a child with remnants of clothes which resembled those worn by a ghostly boy once seen by a young visitor in the room.

As I grew older I became less attuned to the phenomena although we would sometimes be disturbed during the dark hours by a noise like buckets hurtling down the front stairs. Some said that this could be the clatter of knights in chain-mail. A visitor to the house once saw a woman standing by his bed but, although the sighs I heard may have come from her, I never saw her myself.

In the Big House, when I knew it, cold was ever-present in the winter and it is one of the most vivid memories of my childhood. Chapped hands, with their sore stinging feel, nearly always accompanied the frosty weather, this in spite of my being warmly dressed in wool vest, liberty bodice, fleecy lined knickers, woollen socks, jersey and serge skirt. Chilblains also were a torment, even when rubbed with a cut onion which was guaranteed as a cure. It is probable that the humble cottager kept warmer in the winter than we did; there was always warmth around the open hearth and none of the small number of rooms was very far removed from it. In the Big House, however, there was no form of central heating and possibly only one of the several reception rooms would regularly have a fire. In the case of illness, wood would be laboriously hauled to the top of the house and a fire lit in the sufferer's bedroom. The soft sounds of the crackling timber were a companionable accompaniment to drowsiness, but when a log dropped lower in the grate and the flames leapt up, fearful shadows shot across the dark room leaving vacant corners where lurked one knew not what. Without electricity there was no question of switching on a heater for instant warmth. The house depended upon a constant supply of wood during winter, and in the yard the cross-cut saw and hefty axe would keep the men busy in cold weather when little other work was possible.

The family butcher delivered the meat every week by pony and trap. It was generally a large leg of mutton, some stewing meat and a 'pluck' for the dogs. Once, arriving home in the brougham from church, as we trundled along the drive, stopping as usual to open the four different gates, we saw the dog charging along the home field. It had the Sunday joint in its mouth and was followed by a panting and furious Eggie.

A visit to Limerick was quite an occasion and prepared for with due seriousness. Shopping there was easy and relaxed. A list was simply handed in to the family grocer who, with beaming face and ingratiating manner, would pack up everything and carry it out to the waiting vehicle, probably with a Peggy's Leg or two or other mouth-watering sweets if I was there. In the draper's, chairs were brought and goods displayed before us with every attention and variety of choice.

When we shopped in the village of Adare the process would be much the same. Usually a messenger would be sent on a bicycle for these 'messages', but from time to time Jenny and I went in by donkey trap. We had many adventures when we did this during the time of the 'Troubles'. There were often trees across the road or hidden road traps to be circumvented. All the same, we were most scared on the occasion when, passing a ruined cottage at the bottom of a steep hill, a disreputable tramp tried to get into the trap. The poor old donkey had never trotted so briskly up that hill as he did that day! We usually loved these trips and the sweet biscuits we munched on the way home.

Mrs Egglestone, a remarkable woman of sterling character, was really the power behind the scenes in the Big House. She was a north country Englishwoman born and bred who had been 'in service' from her earliest days and eventually found herself as housekeeper of the

Divinity Hostel at Bishop Auckland. She was asked one day to fill a temporary vacancy in the staff at Curragh Chase, which must have seemed to her far away. This she was delighted to do as she had made a disastrous marriage to a drunkard. With her little daughter Jenny she set off and so fell in love with her new home that she never returned to her unsatisfactory husband and remained at Curragh Chase for the rest of her life. In her position as cook-housekeeper she had plenty to do. When the family were at home she exercised her considerable ability as a cook and when they were away, as was often the case, she had complete charge and responsibility. She meant a great deal to me as a child and I was never happier than when in her company, usually playing with Jenny.

Eggie always put me in mind of a vigorous Rhode Island Red hen searching around for suitable morsels as she busied herself observing every detail and correcting every fault. With her round, bustling appearance and sandy hair, she was typically north of England, outspoken and undemonstrative but a faithful friend and honest as the day. She thought nothing of sleeping alone with her daughter in the small basement room they shared in that great house, which had the reputation of being one of the most haunted in Ireland. The people of the English north country are steeped in superstition, the effect of which is somewhat tempered by their natural common sense; in the Irish countryside and within the house she found it quite natural to take such things as ghosts or even 'little people' in her stride. She kept the house and its lovely furniture in spotless condition and the family or visitors could come at any time entirely without notice and find everything ready.

There were always men passing in and out of the yard at their work, and Eggie sometimes visited the Protestant steward and his wife at the gate lodge; otherwise she had few intimate friends. Her chief recreation was to wander through the grounds, and there was no one better than her at finding the hidden bird's nest or the elusive fern.

She knew where the best hazel-nuts would be or in which warren black rabbits appeared from time to time.

Calling a doctor was quite an undertaking and Eggie dosed all and sundry with castor oil if they complained of stomach pains. She had other cures, too, and I clearly remember sitting by the fire with a hot onion held to my ear when I had complained of an ache in that organ. It cured it and I never had one afterwards. When one considers that there was no television, no radio and very poor transport, it is amazing how content she was, with an occasional trip to the village for messages or to church on Sunday as practically the only diversions. The two dogs, Patsie and Ranger, were her constant companions and along with the hens and strident guinea fowl enlivened the place. In old age she was to retire to a cottage in the grounds, having devoted the best part of her life to serving Curragh Chase faithfully.

Eggie belonged to the old school of domestic service. She was determined to keep her place as she considered it to be and never presumed to establish an intimate friendship with her employers. At the same time she was a wise counsellor to her mistress and the training she gave the young maids rendered them much sought after as wives later on. She was proud of her position of authority, unashamed of the word 'servant', and the salt of the earth. Eggie was alone in charge through most of the years of the Irish 'Troubles', and I was with her for part of the time. She never asked what side they were on but fed any fugitive that turned up at the door. Many a one slept in the outside loft or stabling but they always fell in with her wishes not to enter the house and risk its being burnt or damaged. On one occasion the IRA did take over the house during the Civil War period, and shortly afterwards the Free Staters set up a machine-gun emplacement on the other side of the lake. There might have been a very destructive attack had not the occupiers of the house slipped away into the woods by the back entrance.

The extensive woods surrounding the estate were ideal hiding-places for the contestants in the Civil War. If, while walking along the woodland paths, the forms of men could be seen darting behind trees in a Robin Hood fashion, one always looked the other way. It was dangerous if they suspected that they had been recognized, and one of them could easily be the herd, ploughman or gardener whom one met every day. Once when Jenny and I were catching the donkey in the paddock, an open lorry came bumping down the ill-kept drive. It was full of noisy, shabby men who amused themselves by tossing hand-grenades up into the air and catching them again in what they hoped was an intimidating manner. They were otherwise polite and well behaved.

The officer in charge informed us that they were sleeping rough in the woods and had come to collect mattresses. Eggie did not argue but led them to the servants' quarters where they collected as many as they wanted and drove off. The officer signed for the mattresses and from his name we later discovered that he had previously been an officer in the British army. At an earlier stage in the history of this unfortunate period, at a time when all nationalists made common cause against the rulers of the country, a party of British soldiers entered the house and proceeded to search for fugitives at the same time as a number of IRA men in the basement, half starved and tired out after being 'on the run' for over a week, were hastily snatching a modest meal of bread and butter. Anxious to avoid a confrontation, someone managed to conduct them out the back door and along infrequently used paths until they finally rejoined their comrades in the deep concealing woods.

The Black and Tans, an auxiliary force brought in by the British to supplement their forces, were the chief ruffians and were quite active in our area. They were called Black and Tans because of the colour of their uniforms. They showed little discrimination and were responsible for many deeds of pure hooliganism. When

travelling to Adare in the donkey trap Jenny and I were
more nervous of meeting them than the Irish fighters.

We were always on the watch for camouflaged ditches dug across the road. It was easier to do that in those days when most of the roads were not as well surfaced as they are now. Trees would also be felled across the road. Both these activities were undertaken by the Irish guerillas to slow down and render easy ambush targets any army contingents that might be passing that way, and they had very good information as to when this was likely to occur. Bridges were frequently mined but some carefully concealed person always remained not far off in order to alert any civilian passing by. The Church of Ireland rector was once called out in the dark late hours to minister to a very ill parishioner who lived some way off. This involved crossing the bridge which is just beside the Rectory. Suddenly, as he pedalled his bicycle in that direction, a man waving a lantern appeared and warned him that the bridge had been mined. In view of the urgency of the case and the respect for all clergy which was a feature of Ireland at that time, the mysterious apparition carefully led the rector between the two points where the mines had been laid. On his return journey he took a longer but less hazardous route.

On one occasion a skirmish broke out five miles away in Adare and we climbed on to the flat roof of the house to see what was going on. Powerful guns were being fired but little damage inflicted. The combatants were, however, 'trigger-happy' where snipers were suspected and the unfortunate cook of the hotel put her head out to see if all was quiet and had it blown off. As a result of the disturbance, although it did not last long, a gaggle of people turned up at Curragh Chase demanding accommodation. 'What?' said Eggie, 'Sleep in this dreadful house? The ghosts have me scared stiff. I would never sleep a single night here but I have a room in the house of the herd and his family.' The people retreated and found all quiet on their return to Adare.

One night from my upstairs bedroom I heard a commotion going on outside and looking out of the window I saw a crowd gathered in altercation. Some had with them tin cans of paraffin oil and were pointing at the house. I heard afterwards that the IRA had come to burn it down as they had done to so many other great houses, but the local people stopped them saying that the de Veres had always been good landlords. The crowd dispersed and the life of the farm and estate went on as usual.

We were indeed lucky as many lovely old houses and their priceless contents were burnt and destroyed by a frenzied peasantry who had long sought the division of the land and who looked upon the large land-owners as firmly allied to the colonial British, as indeed they were in most instances. Now an established and secure government is more anxious to preserve the many-faceted features of Ireland's history.

We kept no car in my early days and the journey to church on Sundays was in the brougham, so like a cab in appearance. Dinny, the ploughman, donned his Sunday best and, sitting on the box in the front, became the coachman. When we arrived in Adare, the horse was unhitched and led to the stable behind the church. We went in to the service and Dinny went down the road to Mass. Sometimes if bent on a pleasurable outing in the summertime we travelled by sidecar or jaunting car, an excellent way to see the countryside.

My father's mother, old Mrs de Vere, lived at The Lodge, Enniskerry, in County Wicklow and I used to go and stay with her occasionally for long periods at a time. She was a tiny old lady but a tremendous character. It was no bed of roses living with Granny as her discipline was even more rigid than that of my parents. 'Army discipline' is what she believed in! No 'arguing' (as she called it) was tolerated.

Granny's three cousins ran a unique handweaving business, Avoca Handweavers, also in County Wicklow.

Emily, Winifred and Veronica, sisters who were to remain unmarried, were rather remarkable women. Emily was tall and beautiful, like an old picture, especially when she wore her lace collars. Winifred was shorter and stocky, very charming and a great gardener. Veronica was clever, artistic and rather withdrawn. They inherited a delightful country house called Tigroney near the Vale of Avoca, made famous by the well-known song describing the meeting of the waters there.

The three ladies, however, were not cut out for a life of pure leisure and country pursuits. They were able, gifted and full of energy. In the grounds of their property there was an old run-down and disused woollen mill and only one old man in the village knew how to run the machines. The sisters decided to re-establish the mill as a going concern and over a number of years this is exactly what they did. They even brought an expert weaver from Donegal to advise them on restarting this industry. From small beginnings the popularity of their products grew, until finally they sold their tweeds and rugs all over the world. The name Avoca Handweavers is now celebrated.

Emily, the eldest, had a strong visual sense and used this gift to match or blend colours, especially in the rugs which were their speciality. These were mostly small-sized knee rugs which made most acceptable gifts, especially wedding presents, and often found themselves used as warm cot blankets when the baby arrived. Not content with all this industry they called in the village children and taught them to use up the oddments of tweed and wool to make soft toys of an Irish flavour to sell to tourists. These sold very well and I think that the children got most of the profits. The most charming of these little models was a donkey with rider and panniers containing chips of turf across his back. This type of souvenir is quite common now.

As their export market grew, I remember them explaining to me how different countries liked different colour combinations. They said that the Americans were very fond of yellow and the Italians preferred darker colours. I must have been about ten years old when I first visited them with my grandmother, and after her death as I grew up, and even after I was married, they often asked me to stay. There would always be great bolts of tweed in the gracious sitting-room, and after dinner the three ladies would be busily occupied going over the entire length of the material and cutting off any wool which was sticking out. Naturally one had to offer to help. Surrounding the house were very attractive woods and a pleasant garden. Here Winifred, the second sister, grew rare rock plants for which she had a good market.

At one period I spent three years at Enniskerry. I had been left in the charge of a governess at Curragh Chase, but she was a retired missionary and preferred to leave me to run wild while she wandered round the neighbourhood addressing meetings on the advantages of converting the heathen. On hearing of this, Granny decided to take me in hand herself. A long-suffering teacher would bicycle from Bray three afternoons a week, while on alternate afternoons I worked on my own. We would sit in the dining-room wrestling with French verbs in *Livre Rouge* or the mysteries of English parsing and analysis, including that confusing and extraordinary creature, 'extension of the predicate'! I have never yet managed to come to terms with this elastic phenomenon. The teacher had much to put up with as Granny had her own antiquated ideas about education and constantly interfered.

In the summer Granny did not believe in complete idleness and 'holiday tasks' or some form of lessons were given by herself. Even when it was not holiday time she made me learn an entire poem every day, no paltry single verse, except perhaps in the case of such monumental works as Macaulay's *Lays of Ancient Rome*. On Sundays it was a case of a whole hymn and the Collect for the Day. I never play the piano now although a lot of money was spent on my tuition. It was not exactly conducive to a love of the instrument playing endless scales and arpeggios on icy mornings or, if a well-known piece was finally mastered, to be told that I was thumping or otherwise ruining it for the listener.

The daily routine was Spartan too, but kept me in excellent health. It started with a cold bath at all seasons of the year, followed by a period of piano practice in a stone-cold room with old-fashioned, knitted cuffs (or mittens) on my hands. I was given two pence a week as pocket money, of which one went to the church collection every Sunday. The other I would save up, seldom buying sweets although occasionally the servants took pity on me and slipped me a bar of chocolate. Once I remember receiving a large box of chocolates for Christmas and looking forward with anticipation to the one that would be doled out every day after lunch, until to my chagrin Granny said, 'Joan, I think we will cut those chocolates in half. They will last longer that way.' I did, however, have my own way of satisfying my cravings for something sweet. One of the sideboard compartments held a large bowl of that delicious type of soft brown sugar in which large 'gooey' lumps could be found, and I would often raid it in search of these.

In spite of these disadvantages I was fond of Granny and she had a great influence on my early years. I made my own amusements and was comparatively happy. I rode a donkey side-saddle along the quiet country roads, every now and then interrupted by the fact that the animal suddenly deflated itself with a loud noise and the cumbersome saddle (with me on it) would swing under the animal's belly. I had two guinea pigs, Timothy and Sarah, whom I took for quite long walks attached to leads, and occasionally I had the bonus of discovering a number of small replicas of them in the hutch in the morning. These I would sell in one of the pet shops which, along with many other interesting little businesses, could then be found lining the Dublin quays.

The mainstay of the household were the two maids, Kate and Maggie, and outside was James, the man of all work. These three really held the reins but never let the 'mistress' realize it. The latter was careful to the point of meanness. Foodstuffs were locked in containers to which Granny had, as she believed, sole access, thanks to a bunch of keys that she always attempted to keep hidden. The bunch of keys was frequently lost, and Maggie would rush around looking under the carpet or the pillows or inside a vase until she found it, being familiar with all the hiding-places! Every week Granny doled out the supply of tea and sugar from the tall 'caddy' which stood on its pod in the corner. This tea was from no ordinary packet such as we now use but would be a mixture of several well-known selected varieties, shaken and blended together on a newspaper. A box of matches, when given out, would have the date marked on it to be shown when another was needed. One had visions of Maggie struggling to light the fire with a single match in true boy-scout fashion!

There was no electric light and in the dark evenings we read by the light of an oil lamp. There were three sitting-rooms and each had a fire lit on successive days. If the dining-room was unheated Maggie would appear before supper-time in the sitting-room with a bundle of shawls and a packet of hairpins. Everyone, including possible male guests, wrapped a shawl around their shoulders, fastening it with a hairpin. Then Maggie picked up the lamp and carried it ahead of us to the dining-room, while we solemnly processed after her, looking like participants in some pagan Festival of Light.

In the drawing-room was a lovely old-fashioned davenport with the usual line of small drawers down each side. Granny had an ingenious and, in my opinion, very sensible method of keeping accounts. The money, bills, etc., which she received or kept for any activity which involved finance, were lodged in separate drawers labelled under different headings. It was therefore only

necessary to go to the suitable drawer when she wanted
money.

Clothes were a cause for apprehension. Granny greatly disliked delving into that davenport drawer marked 'Joan' and dressed me in an odd assortment of old-fashioned garments including hats which she herself had discarded, so that it is really to the credit of our friends in the village that they managed to keep straight faces when I encountered them, but I think I had their sympathy. To crown it all I was allowed no mirror in my bedroom and was obliged to adjust my garments, such as they were, from my reflection in the much-blurred panes of glass in the outside porch; if noticed, even this was greatly frowned upon.

The Sunday church-going could lead to much embarrassment as we sat in the front pew. If we arrived early, as the congregation began to assemble, Granny would go in for private prayer in a voice which gradually increased in volume as she proceeded so that the astonished congregation would be treated to her supplications to the Almighty that she might have patience with the misdemeanours of Joan, who was sitting beside her complete with a strange-looking contraption perched on her head.

Whenever I see a bull, even to this day, I am reminded of the experience I had once while in Enniskerry. In those days there was no question of sex education for the young. One was never told anything, though one was expected to behave with the discretion which accompanied any experience which might touch on this 'hush-hush' subject.

I was playing in the yard one day when James appeared leading a large and lusty bull by the cord attached to its nose. 'Run away,' he shouted, 'this bull is dangerous.' I ran off in haste into the house and up to the window overlooking the yard to observe at a safe distance what this large and alarming animal was doing. I only observed it disappearing into the cowhouse out of sight. I was noticed at the window and told by both Granny and the staff that my behaviour was disgusting and I was more or less 'sent to Coventry' for several days. I was completely mystified and a sudden feeling of something dirty connected with the bull fixed in my mind. It was only after several days that it apparently dawned on the adults that I was completely ignorant of the facts connected with that function which the bull was intended to fulfil.

There was a happier and brighter side to my times at Enniskerry and in the summer, when the children of our friends came home for holidays, I had company and we would roam the fields finding entertainment in many things which might appear dull to the modern child.

I had always suffered from the fact that not only was I an only child but there were also no young cousins or near relatives as neither of my parents had brothers or sisters living. It was while staying with Granny that I acquired the nearest to a sister that I was ever to know. She lived next door at Rosemount and her name was Shana King. She was about ten years my senior, but this made little difference. A brilliant student, she was at Trinity College, where her subject was zoology in which she was later to gain a gold medal, a doctorate and lectureship. She made me her companion on country rambles; together we looked for newts in the old quarry, turned up stones to examine the busy insects that had made their homes in the sheltered darkness, or went after moths by torchlight in the sultry summer evenings which are part of my memories of those days. I developed such a love for even the smallest living creatures that a pet beetle became almost as good as a dog to me when I took him for a walk on my finger and introduced him to the nectar of his favourite flowers. In those early days there was not the present strong feeling against collecting birds' eggs or butterflies, and Shana and I made a considerable collection. It was one of those friendships that are golden to remember and in my most impressionable

years taught me to compensate for frequent loneliness by
a strong feeling of kinship with nature. Shana was later to
die of tuberculosis (like so many others in those days), or
consumption as it used to be called.

There was a lot to admire in Granny's character but
she was not of a warm and affectionate temperament and
indeed for most of my early youth I lacked the experience of the enfolding of loving arms which means so
much to a child. It was not surprising that, as I got older,
I developed a rather pedantic and aloof manner which
probably made me appear a frightful prig among my
contemporaries with whom I seemed to have very little
in common. Granny herself was definitely a snob which,
one must remember, was quite common in those days
when 'class' was frequently referred to. She would not
let me join the local Girl Guides and, absurd as it seems
today, considered anyone connected with trade or business
definitely *déclassé*. To those whom she would consider to
be lower class she was often kind and considerate in her
own way, and I remember she used to give away free to
anyone who came some kind of pill which she considered good for rheumatism. She had no time for the
political 'rebels', as she called them, except to consider
that, if caught, they should be horsewhipped.

Probably the most pleasant times were the winter
evenings when, by the glow of the brass lamp, she would
read to me from the novels of Sir Walter Scott which
she picked up one by one in those little bookshops along
the Dublin quays. I would listen entranced to the exploits
of Saladin, Richard Coeur de Lion, Ivanhoe or Guy
Mannering, while I made a pile of 'spills' out of old
letters. These were used for lighting candles from the
flames of the fire. Eight o'clock was bedtime and only
ten minutes was allowed for the operation of getting into
bed. After that Granny would come upstairs and be quite
nifty with the cane she kept in my room if I were not
already in bed. Many a time I leapt into bed half-
undressed with the clothes pulled well up to my neck

while Granny knelt at my bed and completed the evening ritual by saying some form of versification, ranging from poems such as that written by Cowper about his cat, to the devoutness of the hymn beginning 'There is a fountain filled with blood'.

That newfangled wonder, the wireless, was by now in a number of homes and sometimes we would pause from our session with Sir Walter Scott to listen to it. Granny would perch herself on the music stool with her face almost touching the contrivance from which came the disembodied voice. At times the opinions voiced were altogether too much for her. Such sentiments had never been uttered in her house before and she would switch off the sound indignantly exclaiming, 'Rubbish, rubbish, none of that here.' She greatly resembled a cartoon which appeared in *Punch* about the same period. An old lady was sitting in front of the wireless with a furious expression, remarking indignantly, 'I won't have this man in my house!' and switching the instrument off.

In the summertime we would sometimes travel by pony and trap to visit relations or friends. By the Scalp and Sally Gap we would go even as far as Carrickmines, where Granny was very friendly with the brother and sister-in-law of the famous artist William Orpen. The chief attraction of that visit to me was their voluble parrot. As we made our way to Coologe Granny would tell me of how Richard, the elder brother whom we were visiting, had also wanted to study art but his father forbade it and so he took up architecture. Apparently when it came to the younger son William, who had the same ambition, the father relented.

One of the artist's pupils told me what a wonderful teacher and perfectionist he was. As an eager and anxious youth this man first appeared in the class with a box containing, among other things, a ruler and an india-rubber. Orpen strolled over to him, picked up the rubber and the ruler and threw them out of the window. 'Now draw the correct line the first time,' he said.

Sometimes Granny and I drove into Dublin; at other times we took the trap to Bray and went the rest of the way by train. Granny was a bit of a menace in Dublin as she paid little regard to the traffic and, as I followed her, I received angry shouts from the not very numerous motorists, who expected me to 'look after the old lady'. We spent ages in the shops choosing, and very often refusing, everything as she was incapable of understanding that fashions had changed since her youth. This applied especially to items for me, and if I were bought a garment it was often outlandish in the extreme. Granny kept her money in a little bag underneath the first layer of her skirts, and an astonished shop assistant would watch as she hitched them up in order to reach it! There was a fine material rather popular at the time called voile, but it was always pronounced as 'voyle' and Granny would insist on pronouncing it in her purest French to the utter incomprehension of the assistant.

Usually Kate the cook accompanied us on these trips. We were allowed only a cup of tea and a bun at the ABC restaurant where we had lunch, but on the way home Kate would call at the village shop for rashers and, as the pony toiled up the last hill, my mind was filled with thoughts of fried eggs, rashers and potatoes.

One of our most delightful outings was the annual visit to Bushy Park in the Terenure area of Dublin. Here lived Sir Frederick and Lady Shaw in a lovely house surrounded by extensive grounds. The family have now long since departed and only the house stands with its community of nuns. The land has all been developed for housing with Templeogue Road following the route of the old avenue. Eleanor, Lady Shaw, a gracious and charming person, was the daughter of Horace de Vere, a son of Sir Aubrey, the 2nd baronet. The name Shaw is now chiefly associated with the famous author and playwright who was not well known at that time. Elderly observers told me that his facial features were typical of the family. Although from a less distinguished branch, it is Bernard Shaw who is now remembered when the glory has departed from the house and grounds of his wealthier relations.

Even in those days the house was an example of the decay which had firmly set in among the landed gentry. It was slightly gloomy inside with massive furniture and carvings, and was run with one maid and the daughter of the house giving valiant help. We sat down at the vast dining-room table where in times past servants in plenty had handed around the dishes. Afterwards the two grand-children and I disported ourselves in the large overgrown garden and gorged on what the birds had left of summer fruits, raspberries, and white and black currants. This trip we had undertaken entirely by pony trap. It was a pleasant outing when the weather was good, and it always seemed to be good. I got plenty of exercise as I was pushed out of the trap at every incline or steep hill in order to relieve the pony of my weight. We dreaded meeting pigs either in a cart or walking to market. The pony had an absolute horror of these animals and would kick up quite severely, obliging me to lead her by the head for quite some distance.

I went for a long walk by myself nearly every day when living with Granny. In the winter I wore a knitted jacket and a large scarf folded across my chest and pinned at the back with a safety-pin of business-like proportions. There were several ways that I could go, but always I passed the forge from which the ring of iron upon iron constantly hit the air. The rounded door, shaped like a horseshoe, stood open revealing the glow within. From the hooves of the horse being fitted there arose an acrid drifting smoke as heat touched hoof. My favourite way was through Powerscourt demesne and its extensive beech-lined avenue which, in places, afforded distant views of the rounded Sugar Loaf mountain.

I would often take a short cut through the Enniskerry Church of Ireland cemetery. There still is, in one corner, a beautiful but sad grave above which stands the marble replica of a charming little girl. The inscription tells us that she died in 1917, 'Dear. Dear. Only child.' One thinks of that sad year when the First World War was raging and countless young lives were sacrificed every minute, and yet to the parents of that little child it was as if they had experienced the sorrows of the whole world. I felt embarrassed as I passed this spot for somehow I identified myself with this child of my own age, but I was still alive, full of joy in the present and hopes for the future. Every morning a bicycle would be parked by the little wicket gate as a quiet woman knelt arranging flowers in a vase. Every day this mourning mother came and prayed at the grave, and if she were there when I passed, I would creep silently by in case the sight of me should intensify her feeling of loss. I recently stood by this grave again and saw that this mother had herself found her last resting-place in this spot. She had died in 1979 aged 102.

Sometimes I took an iron hoop to bowl along the quiet roads, but at other times I was content to observe all that the changing seasons brought in a world my young mind felt had been created especially for me. The autumn was best. I hunted between the toadstools and underneath the beeches for fat and edible nuts and sometimes ventured across the field to gather blackberries to take home for Kate to make into jam. Here butterflies of all descriptions, but especially the blue ones, drank their fill of honey from inconspicuous white flowers, savouring the last of the summer sun.

The wild garden was also a source of delight. In summer all kinds of birds nested there and hedgehogs rustled among the leaves. They were experts at finding the nests of hens that had 'laid out' and especially relished the eggs if they were rotten.

I seldom suffered from illness but if I appeared out of sorts the cure-all was a dose of Gregory's Powder, a particularly unpalatable grey concoction but quite efficacious. A sudden stomach-ache was dealt with by hot milk spiked with plenty of pepper, and if I had a cold linseed would be boiled and the resultant jelly mixed with lemon, which was excellent for a cough.

Those days came to an end but I often think now of that indomitable little old lady, dressed in bright colours and wearing a variety of long earrings bought for her in her girlhood by a doting father. She feared nobody, never complained of loneliness or the ageing process and entered fully into all the activities of the life around her.

She had met many interesting people including Marconi, who was related by marriage to her husband's family as Marconi's wife was the Hon. Beatrice O'Brien, a daughter of the 14th Lord Inchiquin. On a sea journey she met Sir Ronald Ross, whose discovery that the Anopheles mosquito carries malaria was one of the major medical events of the century. He told her that he was on holiday and heartily tired of looking at mosquitoes, but after much cajoling he agreed to show her a slide of the guilty insect under a microscope. Prior to Ross's breakthrough people believed that the source of malaria came from the air or stagnant water, not from the whining flies which did indeed spend their first imma-ture period in such water.

Lucy Wynne, as Granny then was, had enjoyed a happy childhood in Corfu. She had been both born and christened on that idyllic island, an experience shared with Doctor Edith Somerville, co-author of *Some Experiences of an Irish R.M.* and other well-known books. Her father, Lieutenant-General Wynne, was stationed there when, for a period, the British governed that island. Among Granny's interesting recollections of that time was the night her father had been kept awake by strange noises in his bedroom. He got up the following morning to inspect Parade and reached for his smart and spotless uniform. Nowhere, however, could he find his braces. As the bugle sounded he rushed out with a belt as a substitute. On his return he opened a drawer and there, curled round in a circle, were the braces with six pink baby mice inside! He had not the heart to disturb them.

Granny was a brilliant raconteuse and, when friends joined us for supper, they would egg her on to tell one story after another. She particularly liked to relate how, as a young bride living in Connemara, she went with a friend to the local 'fair' in order to buy poultry. Irish was freely spoken in the locality and in order to facilitate their marketing they learned two phrases: 'How much?' and 'Too much'. When they arrived at the bustling scene they drove in their pony trap to the place where red-petticoated and black-shawled women greeted their question 'Cé mhéad?', 'How much?', with vociferous and various shouted retorts. Suddenly, realizing that they did not understand a word, they called out in despair 'Róchostasach', 'Too much'. Pursued for some distance by a crowd of indignant viragos, they whipped up the pony and speedily made their escape.

One time Granny kept house for my father during his first period in the Seychelle Islands in 1910, when my mother had returned to Ireland. Cocktails were then a comparatively new form of tipple. There was a dinner party at Government House and the aide-de-camp asked, 'Mrs de Vere, may I bring you a cocktail?' Never having encountered one before, Granny replied, 'Yes, but please do not give me a full tumbler.' No one, not even her own son, enlightened her on the potency of the beverage she was receiving. Having downed the lot she leaned heavily on the arm of the Governor who was taking her in to dinner and hastily consumed the roll of bread on her side-plate. I imagine that she had something to say to her son, who had clearly been part of the conspiracy, on the homeward journey!

When I returned to Curragh Chase from the three-year visit to my grandmother my parents were back from a stint with the Colonial Service abroad and had settled down to a mild social life. Relations from England were coming to stay, languid, willowy women with drawling voices and imperious ways. I was temporarily forgotten as mattresses were heaved from four-posters and aired, and rooms were opened up which had lain idle for ages. One such was the large bow room in which old Sir Stephen had died. Here it was that he had regularly slept and others, creeping up late to bed, would hear him groaning and talking in his sleep as he dreamt that someone was coming to kill him. This was probably a subconscious trauma from his days on the emigrant ship. From this room he had arisen one night and, still asleep and in his night-shirt, saddled his horse and ridden several miles to the home of his cousin, Lord Monteagle, at Mount Trenchard near Foynes. This room was generally unused but, along with others, was once more occupied.

In a 1921 household which was becoming increasingly austere since the war and the social changes that it brought, I watched fascinated as once more gay evening dresses floated down the winding stairs for dinner. In the morning the little maid carried brass cans of hot water to leave outside the door of each guest. They sought to recover something of the days of their youth, when life for the upper classes was easier. Then, what was now but shadow was a solid reality. Guests were numerous and friends and relations from the county society all around called frequently and were called upon.

In earlier years the hunt met regularly in front of the house. Horses were kept in the loose boxes, ladies climbed on to their side-saddles from the mounting block in the yard and dashing young bloods in hunting pink held life and limb cheap beside the prowess and fearlessness they might display. The hunting scene was very much a part of the social life of county families.

Once the relatives left, things soon settled down to their usual humdrum pace, and for any young person growing up, or even for a child, life was exceptionally dull. There were so many taboos and things that were simply 'not done'. The local country people managed to make their own fun with ballad and story-telling sessions in their houses, or in friendly gatherings on a summer's evening at the crossroads where they danced into the small hours to the music of the local fiddler. Such things were not for the child of the Big House and, indeed, as our own forms of social life declined, there was very little that was.

Those were still the days when the Big House took upon itself (as indeed it was expected to) the various functions now carried out by the government social services, and beggars and various supplicants came constantly to the door. I spent much of my time on errands of mercy to the various cottages. I remember my horror when the illiterate retired gardener, on being presented with a bottle of medicine with a label which said 'Take a teaspoonful three times daily', swallowed the whole lot remarking, 'This will do me good.' Fortunately he appeared to be none the worse. Advice was seldom welcomed, however well meant. One woman, whose babe-in-arms had a virulent and persistent cough, greeted my suggestions that she should seek medical help with 'The nerve of the girl, telling me how to bring up children, and I've buried three of them.'

Many a time supplicants arrived with such remarks as 'Would the Mistress have e'er an old coat of the Master or a pair of shoes?' If available they usually received them and departed showering blessings from the three Persons of the Trinity and every conceivable saint. If not, their curses would be equally vociferous and at this point the steward took a hand and hunted them in no uncertain manner.

The maids became rather fed up when continually asked to offer cups of cocoa to this motley throng, especially as they were sometimes seen to throw it away in disgust. They hit upon an artful, unkind idea and from time to time emptied worm powders, which were kept for the dogs, into the mugs. This certainly lessened the numbers that called the following week!

My parents were never very sociable. They did not entertain a great deal and when living for periods at

Curragh Chase they seldom remained long enough to become assimilated into the regular pattern of the local county society. My father neither hunted nor attended race-meetings and my mother, who never really shook off her somewhat rigid evangelical upbringing, did not always find sympathetic friends among the local ladies. She devoted herself to the care of her more needy neighbours in the cottages around about and no doubt she was often taken in but was prepared to take that risk.

At Curragh Chase we employed a small staff and I enjoyed my first experience of having a maid unpack my luggage and generally attend to me. We maintained a modicum of old-fashioned style; the long-drawn-out dinners in the evening were followed by a lax period with the ladies in the drawing-room while the men remained to chat and drink port after their meal.

On one occasion, in my late teens, my father decided to take me with him on a holiday. Away from home he forgot about being either the important judge or the dignified landlord, and became a most congenial companion and friendly traveller. We went first to Connemara and Achill Island, where he called the red-petticoated peasant women 'Ma'am' and engaged them in long conversations. Together we hunted for Achill amethysts and searched the seas for the giant basking-sharks.

Once we decided to visit cousins living in County Galway. My father's grand-uncle Horace (Frances Horatio de Vere) had married the heiress of the family of Burke of Issercleran, near Craughwell in County Galway, and one of their grandsons, Jim Cole, lived there with his family. My father was seriously considering leaving Curragh Chase to one of Jim's three sons, as it was entailed and he had no real heir. Aileen, the wife and mother of the family, came of a distinguished Scottish line distantly related to Elizabeth, the Queen Mother.

Jim Cole's brother was Horace de Vere Cole, the well-known practical joker. His most famous exploit was his impersonation, while still a student in 1910, of the

Emperor of Abyssinia. He arrived with some friends, his entourage, on a state visit to England, where among other things he was shown over H.M.S. *Dreadnought*, the flagship of the British fleet in Portsmouth, while Edward Prince of Wales, a midshipman at the time, stood at attention as he passed. The government were so embarrassed by the hoax that they never prosecuted Cole, despite the fact that it represented a major breach of national security. It was widely reported in the newspapers as the 'Bunga Bunga Incident' because the imposters set up a cry of 'Bunga Bunga' whenever they wanted to show enthusiasm for the various features of the ship displayed to them.

Horace de Vere Cole was completely unlike the rest of the family, who could never quite make up their minds whether they were ashamed, embarrassed or amused by his jokes. He showed extraordinary creative imagination in devising a series of pranks which are still hailed as being among the great classic practical jokes. He it was who, dressed as a labourer and again assisted by a group of friends, roped off a section of Piccadilly and left lamps, pickaxes and other equipment lying there as if excavation was about to begin. London traffic was disrupted for days until the harassed police force finally realized that no work was actually in progress. Again, it was he who would ask some passer-by in the street to hold one end of a measuring-tape while he took the other end around the corner of a building. Once out of sight of the original victim he would recruit a fresh volunteer to hold the other end of the tape while he made off to a vantage point where he could watch them unobserved. Some of London's most distinguished citizens are reported to have spent hours hanging around street corners as a result of this deception. He came to my parents' wedding – a strictly formal dress affair – wearing a loud check suit, and during the service was heard to comment in a loud voice, 'If I had my way I would abolish the whole ceremony.'

46   In 1955 the Coles sold Issercleran at Craughwell, and it was bought by John Huston, the film director, who called it St Clerans and carried out a number of alterations. Michael Cole, the second son, whom my father finally chose as heir to Curragh Chase, joined the Royal Air Force when war broke out but sadly, having survived the dangers of enemy aircraft, he died when his overloaded plane crashed on his way home on leave in 1953. The estate was then left to Murrough Vere O'Brien, another descendant of Elinor de Vere and the Hon. Robert O'Brien.

From an early stage I was keenly aware of being cut out of the inheritance because of my sex. Curragh Chase had been entailed for generations, and although after my father's death it would probably have been possible to break the entail, my mother would never have done so. I loved Curragh Chase dearly and, ironically, in later life became the only person in the family who continued to really care about it.

In 1925, not long after this visit to Galway, my father accepted an offer from the British Colonial Office to go to the island of Cyprus as a District Judge. Bags were packed and affairs set in order, and Curragh Chase was once more left to the careful guardianship of Eggie.

THREE

'Out Foreign': Cyprus, the Seychelles and Kenya

THERE WERE three reasons for my parents' decision to take up a posting in Cyprus. Firstly, my father had already held legal positions in far-flung regions of the British empire and would not have had the same opportunities in Ireland. Secondly, the climate in Cyprus was healthy enough for them to take me with them. Thirdly, the large estate of Curragh Chase was, curious as it may appear, a financial drain. There was little income from a property which had for so many years been looked upon as chiefly decorative. Small farmers seemed able to make a reasonable living, but the large estates were not as yet organized along business lines.

My mother was a poor housekeeper at home and quite unable to cope abroad, so my parents took with them a housekeeper called Flossie Tucker. She was a native of Kent and had been employed for years as a stewardess on the Orient Line before spending some time in Australia. This had left her with a very marked accent. She was sufficiently plain for my father to remark that he felt her virtue could never have been in danger during her period of shipboard life.

Flossie was put in charge of me in recognition of her brief experience as a children's nurse in India. I was now about thirteen years old and well developed for my age. The cult of the teenager had not yet evolved and I was treated completely as a 'child in the schoolroom', as the expression was. This was an amorphous period from which the upper-class young girl was allowed to escape at around seventeen to eighteen years of age, at the stage known as 'coming out', when restrictions were suddenly removed.

Life was fun aboard the ship which took us on the first part of our journey. We played quoits and shuffleboard on the wide deck, enjoyed a large choice of unusual dishes in the dining saloon, and spent quiet times in a deck-chair watching the sea.

On arrival at Port Said I was firmly struck by the impact of the East. Everywhere were jostling, long-robed crowds, veiled women, beggars, hawkers, and always the heat.

We picked up a very different kind of ship the next day to take us to Cyprus. The passengers were strange and the accommodation poor, while in the dining saloon the table manners were unusual. Breakfast was accompanied by loud slurping noises as passengers sucked a succession of very lightly boiled eggs.

We landed at Larnaca and went to spend the first couple of nights with the local District Commissioner. As I lay in the cool, tiled bedroom, which I shared with Flossie, I experienced homesickness for the first time. It was not that I had left behind anyone particularly dear to me, but the extraordinary feeling of severance was stronger in those days of slower travel; and how acute it was, penetrating one's whole being like a sharp knife, a sensation exceeded only by the pain of lovesickness. Soon, interest in the new country and the journey by battered Ford to Paphos, our destination, quite took over the senses. Fields bloomed with anemones, wild tulips and asphodel, and orchards flowered with peach and apricot, while the constant flocks of sheep and goats jingled by, led in true gospel style by a caring shepherd.

Until our own house was ready, we put up at the local 'Rest House' whose caretaker was a dapper little Turk called Mustapha, a name popular at that time when Mustapha Kemal, the head of a new and revolutionary government, ruled in Turkey. Our Mustapha doubled as the local barber and his services were in great demand by everyone, including the District Commissioner. He informed us of his offices to this gentleman one day when he rushed off 'to cut the hairs of Mr Brown'.

Before long our house was completed. It was a lovely old Turkish building enclosed behind high walls to prevent strange eyes from observing unveiled women in the garden. The garden was perfumed by orange blossom and jasmine, and brightened by zinnias and clumps of lilies. The house itself rested on a series of arches and above it was a flat roof-space where it was possible to sit and watch languid camels stringing their way from the countryside laden with baskets of figs, grapes, melons and other delicious fruit.

A Turkish Bath stood opposite our house and its proprietor frenetically chopped wood in order to stoke his furnaces. He would often start up before dawn broke and my mother, a poor sleeper, would lean out of a bedroom window and protest. 'Keep quiet! Shut up!' she would yell, but alas he understood no English, or possibly his strongly Muslim soul was so shocked to see a female figure in a flimsy night-gown hanging out of the window that he could think of nothing else. At any rate he continued regardless.

I had joined the Parents' National Educational Union, usually known as the PNEU, a well-known correspondence school system, and I would regularly send off exam papers to England where they were marked along with those of hundreds of other children from many different parts of the world. Two hours a week a Greek teacher would give me and William Brown, the Commissioner's son, a Latin lesson, arriving with a beaming smile and the remark, 'How are the boys today?'

Zoë, the daughter of a Greek bank manager, was my great friend. We were of the same age. She was motherless and had an Irish governess, Miss Dowling, so she consequently spoke excellent English. We giggled and whispered together as we sat under the plumbago arch in the garden. Flossie Tucker was often the subject of our merriment, although she could be no joke. She would cut a large number of slices of the heavy local bread and insist that I eat them all, at the same time remarking, somewhat inaccurately, that I had a figure like a sack tied in the middle. Every week, whether or not I needed it, she would administer a dose of calomel followed by Epsom salts. She had a pile of white cotton stockings left over from her stewardess days and these she sold to my mother for my use. They were already well worn, and I was continually darning them.

The servants that we employed included a male cook (who perpetually suffered from sore eyes in the pokey, smoke-filled outdoor kitchen), a maid, and an occasional chauffeur-cum-valet who would go with my father when he visited Limassol, which was also under his jurisdiction.

The plumbago festooned with delicate blue the arbour where we sat every morning in summertime. Roses added a delicious perfume and contrasting pink to the scene, and pomegranates hung from the bushes all about. We were gathered for the simple religious service that my mother held every Sunday as we had no church or chaplain of our own denomination in the little town of Paphos. Reading the simple gospel stories in a setting not unlike the garden that Christ himself often visited, the familiar text came to life. We also had our own primitive well. Doves and sparrows busied themselves among the trees; the dust of the road disturbed by the feet of donkeys and camels flew over the garden wall; and, not far off, golden corn ripened in the fields or, if it were spring, anemones or 'lilies of the field' spotted the grubby grass with bright patches of colour.

Perhaps, however, the most biblical aspect of Cyprus was the rugged shepherd with his flock of sheep or goats. The sheep knew his voice and would follow no one else, and at night he lay across the open entrance to the field where he corralled his flock as darkness fell. Disputes over sheep were common in the cases that came before my father. One seemed impossible to settle, so, remembering some of the judgments of Solomon, my father said, 'Bring the sheep here. Now let each of you call it.' It answered one call only and the judgment was easy to make.

Our little family was joined by Zoë and any other summer visitors who cared to take part in our garden service. Zoë's own Church was Greek Orthodox but she joined in most of our activities. It was truly a case of 'Where two or three are gathered together'. We lived in a largely Turkish quarter, and even as we held our Christian service, the far-reaching call to prayer would ring out from the tall minaret of the mosque just a stone's throw away. In those days this involved a long climb to the top for the man whose duty it was. Now it is often a loudspeaker which relays the message.

The dignified Turkish judge, Raif Effendi, had a charming little daughter called Neriman who came to visit me from time to time. It was not easy to communicate as she spoke little English and we got no further than her teaching me to count up to ten in her own language. A spirit of modernism was growing but had not yet firmly taken hold. Most of the Turkish men still wore the red fez which I must confess looked very smart. Once or twice, Neriman took me into the labyrinthine heart of her home where her mother and other women remained veiled and, to a certain extent, confined by their own wish. Change was not easy for the older generation, and when Neriman grew up she probably became one of the many emancipated Turkish women.

Beautiful beaches were within easy distance but, curiously enough, no one went bathing. In the hot season we usually roamed in the hills along twisted forest paths where hares ran through fragrant undergrowth and the occasional small snake joined lizards basking on the sun-soaked stones.

Food was cheap and varied and I especially enjoyed the rich goats' milk, yoghurt and cheeses. There were fruit and vegetables in abundance and at the time a huge round basket of figs or grapes could be bought for a few pence. In spring the countryside exploded with wild flowers, but later on, as dryness took hold, blindfolded donkeys described monotonous circles around local wells drawing water for irrigation.

I had great fun one summer keeping silkworms. Silk production was common then and most roads were bordered by mulberry trees. I bought eggs, which quickly hatched, and soon elephant-grey caterpillars were receiving a large supply of mulberry leaves twice a day and could be heard munching away in the shed where they were kept. Afterwards, supplied with brushwood, they spun their intricate cocoons, and when I took these to the filature, or silk factory, I received back a 'golden fleece' of yellow spun silk.

The many Greek Orthodox monasteries acted also as hostelries where we sometimes stayed. There was one well-remembered occasion when the ubiquitous Flossie and I spent several days as guests in one. By this time I was aged about fourteen and soon noticed that one of the long-haired young novices followed me everywhere and constantly arrived outside our room with bunches of wild flowers, to be received somewhat icily by Flossie. It was probably unfair to introduce a young girl into this ostensibly celibate community. Flossie hastily decided to leave; on our journey back to Paphos the young chap was also in the car but any romantic leanings he may have had were rather blunted by his being very sick. On our arrival Flossie rushed in to tell her story and I could hear my father laughing heartily, but the matter was not discussed with me and I imagine that it never occurred to anyone that I was actually aware of having been the love object of this unfortunate youth. I considered it rather mean of Flossie to have mentioned his attentions to the abbot and I have sometimes wondered what happened to him when he returned to the monastery.

On another such visit, the abbot invited us to dine at his table. Roast sucking-pig was a favourite dish. The eyes of this or any other roasted animal were considered great delicacies, and our host, full of solicitude, transferred these titbits from his own plate on to my mother's. Disposing of them unobserved was quite a problem and I shall never know how she did it. While we were there a fair was held on the feast-day of the patron saint, with the usual booths selling cheap trinkets.

The abbot bought me a cross set with quite attractive blue glass and a charm against the evil eye, also made of blue glass with a crude eye form in the middle, an interesting example of the mixture of sanctity and blatant superstition which one often comes across.

Usually, in the long hot summers, we took to the mountain resorts. Troodos and Platres were the most popular, but there were also quiet, less frequented places. I remember one trip on donkey-back through dense pine woods to a little isolated forest hut where we spent three weeks in an atmosphere scented by the numerous aromatic herbs growing underfoot. It was like some extended country picnic, riding the large sure-footed donkeys with the females of our party clad in ridiculous voluminous divided skirts, stopping in the heat of day beside a delightful cascade of cool water to eat our lunch of home-baked bread, hard-boiled eggs and fruit.

The court over which my father presided achieved representative status by having on its Bench members of the three communities. The British judge represented the colonial power and there were the two others, one Turkish and one Greek. It was a top-heavy arrangement but at that time seemed to work well enough. There were Turkish villages and Greek villages, and in the towns the two communities lived side by side. The loud, arresting call to prayer by the muezzin rang out twice a day for the Turks from the tall minarets, and the Greeks gathered in their domed churches where the smell of incense wafted around the worshippers and curious icons received the kisses of the faithful. Greek Orthodox priests, with their hair in a bun under tall black hats, were everywhere to be seen.

If you didn't spot the mosque, the grape harvest always made it possible to distinguish a Turkish village, for the fruit would be drying on the flat roofs to turn into raisins and sultanas. While the Greeks turned the fruit of their vineyards into excellent wine, the Turks were forbidden by their religion to make intoxicating liquor.

In 1910, after three years, the call came once more, this time via Reuters telegram. It said: 'You have been appointed Chief Justice of the Seychelle Islands and are to act as Governor until a new one is appointed.' 'Goodbye Zoë! Goodbye Aphrodite's Isle!'

Over forty years later I visited Cyprus again. Our lovely old house on the outskirts of Paphos had melted into suburbia. Much had changed; bitter strife had divided the island, camels no longer plodded the dusty roads and there were few mulberry trees, but there was Zoë, married to a retired bank official. We had never corresponded but it was as though we had parted only the week before.

The Seychelle Islands are now readily accessible by air, but it was not so in 1930. They could be reached only by ship from either India or Africa (they are almost equidistant from both continents), and so once more we left via Port Said for warmer regions. My father was in such a hurry to take up the position to which he had been assigned that he took no home leave in between.

From Egypt we travelled by a luxury P & O liner bound for Bombay. Numerous officials of the British Raj walked the decks and gentle ayahs minded their children with devoted care. In the dining saloon we were served delicious curry with all its concomitants.

We had only two days between ships to be touched by the magic of India. Port Said may have appeared exotic, but Bombay was much more so. There were so many shades of brown in the faces of the crowd, lovely Parsee women in gorgeous silk saris shopped in the stores, while a snake-charmer sat playing his flute outside our hotel. By contrast, up Malabar Hill vultures sat about in gorged and macabre repletion from the corpses exposed on the 'Towers of Silence'.

It was on this voyage that I came across a slang expression which is still widely used. On the ships going to India the coolest and most comfortable cabins were those on the port side, shielded from the midday sun.

The opposite was true for the voyage back to England. The richer and more distinguished passengers therefore tended to book their cabins 'port out, starboard home' and the acronym POSH chalked on their luggage thus gave a new word to the English language.

As we approached the island of Mahé in the Seychelle group the scene was unforgettable. White fairy terns swooped down to the sea and small boats with sails of every hue skimmed past us. On the approach to the port, a background of tree-clothed hills stood out against the blue sky.

The ship anchored as usual a little way outside the harbour. The passengers disembarked and my father, dressed carefully for the occasion, stood on the deck and waited. Where was the government launch sporting the Union Jack which had been sent to meet the Acting-Governor? Where was the reception committee? Where indeed were any of the things that he quite naturally expected? At last as dark was falling, as it does with great precipitation in the tropics, a small boat arrived alongside with the island's medical officer, whom my father already knew. He had some startling news for us.

The Governor had died some months previously and the Colonial Office had appointed a new one who was due to arrive by the next boat. The Chief Justice, a man called de Vaux, was due to leave on our arrival but, relishing the position of Acting-Governor, he refused to do so until the new Governor came. My father, who had been given to understand that he was urgently needed to act as Governor in this interim period, found himself in a very strange position. Furious cablegrams were sent off to London by both parties and feelings ran very high. In the meantime where were we to put up? Instead of the 'red-carpet' reception we had expected, the kind-hearted doctor accommodated us in one corner of the maternity hospital and cries of new-born Seychellois were our first welcome to the islands. The stalemate continued until the new Governor actually arrived. The 'de Vaux-de

Vere' débacle is still spoken of in Mahé, and an account of it can be seen in the local records.

In those days the Seychelle Islands were comparatively isolated and dependent on the mailboat and a large cable station for communication with the outside world. We had a modest but beautifully situated bungalow at the top of a hill overlooking the small harbour, with the sea stretching out to meet the horizon.

From there I set out on horseback every morning to the convent school in the little town. The Indian *syce* (or groom) walked beside me and brought the animal down again in the evening for my return journey. The nuns of St Joseph of Cluny were kind but old-fashioned, greatly concerned with the length of their pupils' skirts and the necessity of keeping 'the human form divine' as well concealed as possible. (I remember bringing an unclothed doll for one of their charities and the horror with which the nun immediately seized a duster to cover it up!) The vivacious French-speaking girls who were their pupils were not particularly concerned with this advice! Gathering in groups was greatly discouraged. I feel the worthy nuns feared that we were discussing matters concerned with that disgusting subject – sex.

My father and I walked for miles all over the island where cars were as yet unknown. On the lower coastal road sedan-chairs plied up and down amongst the horse-drawn traffic. There were fields of the vanilla orchid and of patchouli, used in perfume, and red crabs scuttled from the shoreline on to the road. Up the hilly country road rich tropical vegetation of every kind grew and it was indeed a paradise, as tourists of a later period were to discover.

When slave-trading was pronounced illegal, a great number of Africans were removed from slave-ships and set at liberty on Mahé, where their descendants live to this day. On my parents' previous posting to the Seychelles (my father had held a junior post there in his younger days), they had an old cook who clearly remembered his

father telling him of his capture by Arab slave-traders.
He drew some remarkable pictures of this event. The
Arabs were depicted as tall powerful men and their
victims as small puny creatures. They were probably
more or less all the same size but in the mind of this
African, torn from the security of his own village and
tribe, stature was an indication of power.

It is said that there are probably no original natives of
the Seychelle group. Giant tortoises ruled the land when
the Comte de Seychelle landed there in 1742. The
Seychelles remained a French colony until 1794, when
they were taken over by the British, and formally ceded
to them in 1814. There is a French patois spoken now
among the less sophisticated inhabitants, a relic of those
years. French families, both land-owners and businessmen,
were still predominant on the island and it was the
daughters of the early settlers, some with distinguished
names, whom I met at convent school.

My parents were liberal in their attitude towards my
fascination with all forms of wildlife. I was allowed to
keep a number of interesting pets and Sophie was probably the most attractive of these. She was a brown lemur
brought to me from Madagascar by a school-friend's
father who captained a small trading vessel. She was an
adorable creature and, clinging with her arms around my
neck, accompanied me everywhere uttering her little
cries of 'mac mac!' She had her own house in the garden
and was part of a pet community which consisted of a
booby (a small gannet), a pelican, a giant tortoise brought
from the adjoining island of Aldabra and, later on, an
African monkey. Jacko came from Mombasa in Kenya
and was not a particularly attractive pet as he was capable
of quite a nasty bite which, I did not realize at the time,
could have been dangerous. He was supposed to sleep on
a chair beside my bed, but most nights I would be
awakened by whimpering sounds like a baby's, and then
the noise of the chair being pulled along the ground by
the lead. Soon I would feel something warm settling

down under the bedclothes beside me and in the morning there would be a small damp patch which told its tale. Sophie was up to all kinds of fun and enjoyed riding on the back of the tortoise and playing with the monkey. She would be sitting on the lawn, delicately peeling and munching a banana with her long furry tail stretched behind her. Jacko the monkey would creep up and give it a tweak but when she looked up with indignant 'mac mac's, Jacko would be the picture of innocence.

Behind the house grew great fat avocados which, in season, fell to the ground with juicy thuds while local dogs came in groups to gobble them up. Most islanders, whether French or Creole, were Roman Catholic. Turtles of several kinds were plentiful around the coast and, although they are reptiles and the flesh is not unlike beef, the 'faithful' were allowed to eat their meat on Fridays as early settlers had reckoned that, since they came out of the sea, they must be fish.

We visited the outlying islands from time to time and one of the most interesting was called Cerf after the French word for the deer which had been let loose there, probably as an extra food, and were flourishing. I would hesitate to undertake such a journey now, but I thought nothing of it then.

We set off in a small motor boat and headed straight out to sea until we were in the wide expanse of the Indian Ocean, with my mother cowering in the bottom of the boat. The horizon was eventually broken by a feathery pattern which, as we got nearer, developed into a line of coconut palms behind a broad white beach. The launch stopped some distance from the coral reef and we were each carried on stalwart shoulders across the surf and deposited on the shore.

Copra was the chief industry on Cerf Island, and there were great piles of drying coconut kernels everywhere. We had been lent the manager's bungalow and lived quite well off tinned provisions, including Cow & Gate milk, and a variety of edible and colourful fish. There were corals of every hue along the beach, including blue which I never saw elsewhere, and a number of long shark backbones which could be used as walking-sticks. Large, rather revolting sea-slugs, or 'bêches de mer', were caught by the fishermen and dried for export to China where they were greatly relished.

I returned from the island with a box of scorpions I had collected. The crew of two with their bare feet took a dim view of this in case any should escape, and when afterwards I showed them to Jacko, the monkey, who had probably never seen one before, he ran away gibbering with fright.

During our time in Mahé we took a holiday to Kenya where our visit was protracted due to my mother's being hospitalized for a short period. I was confirmed alone in Mombasa Cathedral and then, leaving my mother to recover, I took off with kind friends in the famous train which runs through the game reserve, then more populated with animals than now. One's eyes were kept glued to the window. Lolloping herds of wildebeest thundered past. Zebra tossed their heads and trotted away. Antelope grazed the low herbage and the odd giraffe plucked leaves from the topmost branches of trees. In the far distance there was a dark and moving cloud reminding us of the swarms of locusts which members of the Agricultural Department spent all day fighting with every known means. When the train stopped we sometimes heard the roar of a lion. Conservation was not greatly considered in those days, nor was it as necessary as now. There were many big-game hunters and numerous lions were shot.

I finally found myself with relations who kept a hotel in what was then known as the White Highlands at a place called Limuru. I really enjoyed myself there and even attended school for a short time. At night there was fun and dancing at the hotel and it was a case of 'when the cat's away'. The hotel was a delightful and popular spot, and grew beautiful scented violets for sale. I shared with the daughter of the house one of the round huts scattered throughout the grounds for the use of guests. She was gay and pleasure-loving and was out most nights at dances.

It was wonderful riding over those open plains, avoiding porcupine holes and passing gatherings of African huts and their dignified red-daubed inhabitants. One felt as free as air in those pre-Mau Mau days. Later on, when fully recovered, my mother came to fetch me and we returned to Mahé and school once more.

It was a great occasion when ships of the British fleet came into the harbour to show the flag. There were parties and dances which, being 'only a schoolgirl' and not 'out', I was not allowed to attend, although my friends were. Once, a German flagship called *The New Emden* arrived but was not warmly received, for the first *Emden* had patrolled these waters in the Great War and inflicted a lot of damage. We made a point of asking the officers up to the house, where they clicked heels and kissed hands in true Teutonic style.

My mother found it increasingly difficult to keep a sixteen-year-old out of the free adult world of which she disapproved. As daughter of the most important official after the Governor, who had no family with him, I was naturally asked to a variety of social functions. She therefore decided to accompany me home to Ireland. A Norwegian cargo ship was in the harbour and, although they did not usually take passengers, they agreed to take my mother and myself and a young Irish doctor called Turner.

I think the rugged captain must have felt that we had mistaken him for Noah when we embarked with Sophie and a tortoise and later picked up a parrot in Port Said. There were already about a dozen outsize tortoises lashed to the deck, bound for European zoos.

The chief steward gave us his cabin and we settled down cosily, enjoying the rich choice of cheeses and other interesting dishes served up at mealtimes. During the day Sophie had the run of the deck and was very popular with the sailors. Finding them gathered round one day convulsed with laughter and neglecting the task of redecorating the ship, I came upon my pet, brush in paw, dipping it in and out of a tin of paint and vigorously licking off the contents. Fortunately she suffered no ill effects.

The chief steward slept in a smaller cabin opposite ours and constantly passed us on the narrow alley-way. He was fat, fair and balding. My protected teenage years and lack of knowledge of the ways of the wicked world had not prepared me too well for the hard facts of life, and although acutely surprised by his searching hands feeling my breasts occasionally as I passed by, I did not understand the language of lust. We were passing through the Red Sea and the heat in the cabin was sweltering, so my mother decided to sleep on the deck for a few nights, leaving me alone with the door open in the cabin. To do such a thing in a ship full of sex-starved men who had not seen their wives or probably any woman for several months, shows what an innocent mind she had. The steward came in from time to time to adjust the porthole, which was quite in order, and seemed to linger around offering drinks of water or fixing the fan. One night I was just going off to sleep when I felt my bunk creaking and two soft fleshy arms reaching up from below as a dim figure tried to heave itself on top of me in the small narrow bed. I pushed hard and screamed, though only faintly aware of what I was screaming about, and the bulky and apparently naked body fell off the bunk and fled through the door. Here I was in a distinct quandary. If I rushed up to the deck myself I had to pass his cabin door, and so I remained awake until daylight fearing to stir. From time to time a long nose appeared in the crack of the door sending me into palpitations, but I learnt afterwards that it had been my mother coming rather too late to see whether all was well.

The steward was confronted with my accusation and naturally denied everything, but I was never again left alone in the cabin at night. In later years, remembering this incident, I considered it likely that this was not the first time that he had entered my cabin with ill intent. The night before he had brought me a drink of water and the following day I didn't wake up until about midday. Had he drugged me and achieved his object unbeknownst to myself? Fortunately there were no unhappy results.

It was a meandering slow voyage of over a month, taking on coal and cargo all along the way and giving me my first sight of the Suez Canal. As mentioned, my mother was not naturally domesticated but we had to do our own washing and, seized with sudden, housewifely zeal, she offered to do the washing of the other passenger, our doctor friend. She scrubbed mightily at a pair of his shorts, afterwards heaving the dirty water over the side of the deck. Alas, she had forgotten to remove the washing. It was a case of emptying out not the baby with the bathwater but the shorts with the laundry water! At the next port of call we went shopping to try to replace them. Somewhat crestfallen by this wasteful washing day, she proceeded to contemplate an ironing spree. We were sitting in the saloon engaged in an interesting argument with the captain when an alarm sounded and there was a smell of burning. A frantic search was undertaken and in our cabin the electric iron was discovered. Having burnt through blanket and table, it had started to tackle the floor.

Finally we arrived at Marseilles and, complete with Sophie in her box and the rest of the menagerie, bade goodbye to the captain, the lecherous steward and the giant tortoises who had been our companions for so long.

Sophie gave great entertainment when she sat with us in an open-air café. A crowd gathered to see her eating cherries and daintily putting up her hand to her mouth to take the stones. No such vulgarity as spitting them out! On the long train journey which took us up through France, the rather starchy fellow passengers kept looking at each other to ascertain who was making such strange noises, until one happened to look up and see a small hairy arm protruding from a square wooden box on the rack.

We boarded ship once more, crossed the English Channel, and arrived utterly exhausted in London, where we took rooms at the Grosvenor Hotel. Propelling the menagerie into the bathroom and shutting the door, we took to our beds. The following morning, rather late, we were aroused by the screams of the chambermaid who had discovered a tortoise in the bath, a parrot swinging from the electric light-shade and a strange little animal which had attempted to hop onto her shoulder.

So it was, after one more sea voyage, that we came back to Ireland. We gave the parrot and the tortoise away to friends but Sophie, dressed in her little red jacket, accompanied me everywhere and was a source of great amusement to everyone she met and to the children of neighbours at Curragh Chase who would come to see her.

FOUR

Stepping Out: London in the Mid-Thirties

CURRAGH CHASE, looked after by the faithful Mrs Egglestone, stood waiting as though we had never left. Granny, though older, was unchanged if more considerate of her maturing granddaughter. It was an even lonelier world now as we had lost touch with so many of our friends. We also had little in common with them now as horses, cattle fairs and shooting parties occupied the minds of most of the men, and the women, although charming as ever, lived in the increasingly shrinking enclave of county society in which trips to coral islands or Red Sea adventures had very little place. Old land-owners, who no longer commanded the respect they formerly had, faced increasing difficulties as smallholders sought to erode their property. All the same, surrounded by the peace of the old house, we felt content although my father was still abroad and my mother would shortly return to him.

Before she went it was decided that I should be placed as a boarder at Alexandra College, Dublin. Poor Sophie had to be sent to the Dublin Zoo where she was, in true Irish style, made very welcome. The local dressmaker was called in to make my school outfit, including the best dress to change into in the evenings. It was of an attractive velvet, but the neck and the general appearance were dull and drab.

Sixteen was rather late to start regular boarding-school, especially for a pupil accustomed to a completely different curriculum and, what is more, it was not easy to adjust to the regimen upon which my family insisted. My mother held strong ideas about the type of conversation engaged upon in dormitories and insisted, at considerable expense, that I should have a room to myself. This, combined with the fact that I had little in common with the other girls, started me off on a completely wrong footing. I knew nothing about the latest films and had no boyfriends to discuss when they gathered in huddles and whispered together. I must have appeared quite a freak, especially when dressed in my dowdy clothes. They knew nothing of the wider life I had lived and were naturally completely absorbed by the carefree trivia of the average schoolgirl. I felt the cold dreadfully, worried about work and finally ended up with a mild breakdown which ended my schooldays.

After a spell with family friends in the north of England, I found myself once again at my beloved Curragh Chase with a dear friend, Jayne Boddy, then in her early thirties, who helped me with quiet study. A parson's daughter from Durham, she had stayed with the family in both Durham and Cyprus. It was utter bliss that winter. At night the leaping flames of the library fire added to the circle of light made by the paraffin lamp as we sat reading aloud beside the desk on which Aubrey de Vere had composed his poems. We were cocooned in an atmosphere of culture. During the day we walked in the frosted woods or joined a friend in her pony trap to follow the hunt at a comfortable distance. On Sundays we went to church, as before. As in all rural communities, the regular Sunday encounters between neighbours were often our main form of socializing and simple plans for tea-parties and other activities were made.

Our nearest neighbours were two charming ladies who lived at Holly Park, an attractive Georgian house. Its woods adjoined Curragh Chase and in those days the easiest approach to it was by a neglected and ill-defined path. On Christmas Day Mrs Egglestone, Jenny her daughter and I set off to have tea and spend the evening with these ladies, carrying two hurricane lanterns to light us on the return journey. The two miles or so took us through a gap in the boundary wall, through the mixed wood, rather nervously through the tunnel of neglected laurels, until we came to the back gate and the straight clear stretch of field to the house.

Coming back was quite different, although warmed by Christmas cheer and carrying generous presents. The two hurricane lanterns shone only on the path in front of us

and the mind enlarged upon the strange sounds of
snapping twigs around us. As we approached the haunted,
neglected cottage half smothered with brambles, where
old Lady de Vere had once taught the local girls lace-
making in the post-Famine years, we huddled together
and slid past, eyes darting in every direction; then past
the wall once more with the blissful stretch of our own
ornamental walk and pleasure-ground to lead us home.

This life-style gave an extra dimension to existence. It
is easy to understand how so many poets and men and
women of letters have sought such a form of living, if only
for a short time. Unfortunately it could not continue, and
change was on the way.

Having discarded the title of schoolgirl, although I
never achieved that of débutante, I was now faced with a
decision about my future. My parents were about to
begin another tour of foreign service. I was not anxious
to return abroad with them at the time so I thought out
a plan. My godmother, Molly Bothamley, lived in Stoke
Newington, London, where she was sub-warden of a
missionary training college. I was devoted to her and, as
she had once been Mrs Moule's private secretary, my
mother knew her well and had complete confidence in
her. I suggested that I should go and stay with her for a
time and this was finally agreed upon. I lodged in the
hostel although I had no intention of volunteering for the
mission field. The students were by no means intimidating. Some were doctors and others nurses and teachers
undergoing a few months' intensive training before
embarking on a missionary career. There were lectures on
all kinds of interesting subjects from Bible study to
comparative religions, and these I often attended. Florence
Allshorn was the Warden and she was an exceptional
person whose writings are still studied and about whom a
book has been written. She was also very human and
although she had already spent several years herself in the
mission field, she was both liberal and enlightened in her
outlook.

The domestic arrangements at the hostel, known as St Andrew's, were managed amicably and the girls engaged in domestic work were called the 'household brigade'. They wore attractive brown dresses and were treated as equals by everyone.

It was realized that in isolated mission stations abroad, far from the nearest doctor, it would be very necessary to have some smattering of medical knowledge and those people who had no experience of these matters were given a 'crash course'. This was at the Islington Medical Mission just a short distance away. It was a surgery and dispensary run on a religious basis. There were several of these medical missions in London at the time and they supplied a definite need. The Islington Mission was staffed by a doctor, a dentist, a nursing sister and a number of students there to gain experience. I decided to join those of my friends who were already working there.

The patients gathered in a large waiting-room and every morning the motley assortment of people sitting on long benches was treated to a religious homily and hymn-singing. The saving of their souls was the main object of the exercise and Christian instruction was integral to the whole organization. It was run almost exactly as a medical mission in some corner of the foreign field used to be, and indeed still is in some places. The staff were, however, thoroughly practical and efficient and the free, or almost free, treatment that they dispensed meant an immense amount to the dwellers in those poorer parts of London before the advent of the Welfare State. The strong religious convictions of the doctor and sister-in-charge had led them to take up posts which were extremely badly paid compared to others they might have had. There were a lot of septic conditions such as boils, ulcers, carbuncles, etc., which we treated with a paste made of Epsom salts. I was a poor hand at giving injections; somehow the needle usually parted from the syringe, earning me a severe reprimand from the sister. Minor operations were also carried out which we observed. There were quite a few cases of discharging ears and while syringing the ear of a patient I once got a great fright when she fell down in a fit. I had never seen an epileptic fit before and I imagined that I had done something wrong.

We would be sent out on the district for minor matters such as giving enemas. It was surprising how often we had to do this and it was not an easy task to carry out in some sordid bedroom where the facilities were not the best. Constipation seemed to be a serious problem and doses of Epsom salts or even castor oil were constantly administered. There were none of the modern ideas about roughage. Most of the men in the houses we visited were working, although their wages were low. Rightly or wrongly, expectations were not high and there was an extraordinary amount of quiet contentment though there was, undoubtedly, a great fear of serious illness. Before the advent of modern drugs, pneumonia, so easily contracted by the undernourished for instance, could be a killer and tuberculosis was a constant dread.

Although poverty in the 1930s was often manifest, it inspired in many a spirit of dedication and service. However, a feeling that 'the poor are ever with us', rather than the modern more positive attitude that something should be done about it, was no doubt prevalent. The state has now largely taken over the type of work that we were engaged upon in the Islington Medical Mission, but they are not so concerned with the souls of the patients.

In the years when I lived in London there were not the same number of dark faces to be seen as have appeared following the break up of the colonial empire. However, a number of families of mixed race lived in the dock areas, where coloured men had married white women, and life was not always easy. The students of St Andrew's worked a lot in the docks, took the children on holiday camps and generally brightened their lives. Near our own neighbourhood I participated in the running of clubs for local girls. In those days before television there was little for the youngsters to do in the long winter evenings, and we sought to keep them off the streets.

When my six months at the Mission were over I enrolled for a Domestic Science course at the Holloway Polytechnic. We worked in pairs and I found myself coupled with a pleasant young nun. The other girls had rather avoided her but in Ireland and abroad I had met many of her kind and it was an excellent arrangement. With the dedication peculiar to her calling, she was a great worker and was always prepared to take on the harder tasks.

I made few friends as I was not a good mixer among my own age-group, having lived so much with those older than myself. Most of the teachers were pleasant enough but I had no liking for the sewing mistress. Real silk was reasonably priced and with it we made some lovely lingerie items and, after one had put some weeks of work into a delicate piece of underwear, she had a nasty habit of coming up behind one, seizing the garment and ripping it from seam to seam, remarking coldly, 'You have a lot to learn!' In spite of all this, I succeeded in obtaining my first-class diploma.

The girls were a mixed group. There was the sulphurous redhead and the lively brunette who never had to pay for her own lunch in the Poly canteen. She showed her appreciation in the knitting of a series of long mufflers, which varied in length and pattern according to the strength of her feeling for the current boyfriend. There was also a slightly retarded girl who wore throughout her activities an anxious and worried expression. She became the butt of the sadistic sewing mistress until one day we were all sobered to hear that she had run away and could not be traced. Fortunately she did turn up later but never appeared among us again.

There was much more to the craft of housewifery in those days than there is now, when a few minutes with the vacuum cleaner or floor polisher often suffices. We made elaborate lists of the duties to be carried out every day and the exact types of brushes and dusters to use. We learned how to make many polishes and cleaning materials ourselves and I remember a very efficacious scouring soap called Monkey Brand. Spring-cleaning duties were a very important matter which we were taught how to tackle with single-minded fanaticism, while any future families that we might have would be left to fend in discomfort for themselves.

Many of the labour-saving devices that we now take for granted were not allowed; others had not yet been invented. Packet this and packet the other had not invaded the kitchen as they did later on. Custard was the genuine thing made with eggs, and anyone thinking of using the powder-made variety would probably have been considered either very lazy or very poor. Tinned foods, especially meat and fish, were definitely suspect and if used had to be removed from the container immediately. Refrigerators were seldom used domestically. There were no washing-machines and very few suction cleaners. Laundry was done by hand. With few male relatives I had little experience of washing, starching and folding a shirt. I obtained one from the brunette, who had several brothers, and managed to master the complicated art of correct folding. The authorities were kind, however, and we all got our diplomas. We were turned out as potential efficient marriage partners and employers of domestic help.

Most of the girls in our group considered marriage to be a career in itself, and indeed there would always be plenty to do. At Christmas we had all made and decorated a cake, and the one which I made in the shape of a crinoline lady was the means whereby my future husband was to hear of my existence. I packed it up and sent it to my parents, then in Grenada in the West Indies. They introduced it at a tea-party to which the Director of Education, a Welshman, had been invited.

It was natural, living in such an atmosphere and having become familiar with the problems of the underprivileged, that I should consider social work as a definite career. With this in view I embarked on a course that I hoped would finally qualify me as a hospital almoner. This old-fashioned term has been done away with now but it meant a link between hospital, patient and home. As the practical part of my training I worked for about a year with an institution bearing the ghastly name of 'The Charity Organization Society'. We travelled all day up and down the Great North Road and the dreary houses of Holloway armed with bundles of forms. In the houses of those looking for help our reception was often hostile as we were considered 'Nosy Parkers'.

The amount of assistance forthcoming depended on the answers to our questions, and assurance had to be given that employment had been sought. This had to be any reasonable job and not necessarily the previous occupation of the breadwinner. As one looks back, it must have seemed a gross impertinence for a young woman who had never wanted for anything to go into the homes of people much older than herself demanding to see the marriage certificate and other documents, and sometimes we got a dusty answer or else were shown the door!

Those were the days of London smog, taken as a matter of course especially in November, and finding unknown houses and addresses was often difficult. Yet there was very little crime and one never had the slightest fear of entering even the darkest alleys.

When my period of practical work was over in north London I had one more test before finally being accepted by the Board of Almoners. I was sent for a day to the social worker side of St Thomas's Hospital. When there I was told to go to a certain address some way off to inform the family that someone belonging to them had died in hospital. No doubt this rather testing mission was especially chosen and I remember how I dreaded the encounter with the bereaved family and sought about in my mind for a suitably sympathetic approach to the sad news. I was very relieved when I arrived at the house to find no one in. I waited for some time and then left a message with a neighbour.

This was apparently the right procedure for I found that I had passed muster on the practical side. However, I still needed to do a year's diploma course at the London School of Economics, but was unable to go as I had never taken the necessary entrance exam. My parents, while providing me with tuition on a variety of subjects, had never considered examinations a necessary preparation for the life that they expected me to lead. Up to this I had not contemplated attending a university and looked upon people with degrees as rather superior beings. My cousin, a girl of average intelligence, went to London University and received her BA, and I always felt inferior to her.

While in London I heard quite by chance of the death of that intrepid character, my grandmother. My parents were abroad and no one had thought of telling me. Forty years afterwards I visited the house in Wicklow once more. There was the little bedroom where I had scurried hurriedly to bed listening for the step on the stairs. There was the bow window where I had sat to learn my lessons and observed the busy life of the yard going on, and there was my own small garden bed with the variegated broom I had planted so long ago.

The long summer holidays were rather a problem for me. I usually went to friends or relatives on what would now be considered an 'au pair' basis. I made myself useful in a quiet way but expected no remuneration. One summer, however, Molly Bothamley and I set off for Ireland in her little Austin 7 Mini called Riki Tiki Tavi. It was great fun explaining unfamiliar landmarks to her as we bowled along at an easy pace. In Dublin we met my dear friend Shana King, whose TB was far advanced and for whom the end was near. She had had to give up her lectureship at Trinity College and she and her mother lived in a small flat in Upper Leeson Street. Afterwards we made our way quietly towards Curragh Chase and I enjoyed the moment when, from the top of the hill, I could show Molly the great stretch of mixed wood and, as we negotiated the winding drive, there was the house with its half-drawn red blinds standing out against the grey stone. Inside the library there was a cosy fire in front of which the table was laid for tea and Mrs Egglestone bustled in with hot, home-baked scones and yellow home-churned butter. The stillness all around us seemed filled with a message of welcome.

About this time my parents came home on leave once more, and after we had all spent the summer at Curragh Chase I decided to postpone further study for a time, buy some pretty light clothes, and return with them for a period to the West Indies, where my father was now Chief Justice of Grenada, southernmost of the Caribbean Islands in the Windward group. This decision was to prove a turning-point in my life.

FIVE

Grenada

GRENADA, in many ways not unlike the Seychelles, is a lovely volcanic island twenty-one miles by twelve, fringed with white sandy beaches. First discovered by Columbus in 1498 and then called Conception, it is now greatly developed as a tourist resort but in the 1930s was comparatively 'unspoilt'. Our house, Mount Wheldale, overlooked the harbour and the red-brick French buildings of a former century. The Governor at the time was Arthur Grimble, who later became well known as the author of *Pattern of Islands* which described his period of service as a young man in the Gilbert and Ellice group in the Pacific, where he delivered one of his several lively daughters in the absence of medical help. His wife rubbed her with coconut oil and left her naked like the native children, which gave her a good skin in later life.

Grenada was known as 'the island of spices' and produced and exported cinnamon, cloves and nutmeg, as well as bananas and cocoa. The moguls of this industry were the Mincing Lane fraternity who controlled the trade. In good times the planters, resident or absentee, squandered their money and seldom helped the local people, who had little representation in the government. When the market was bad retrenchments were drastic. The small relief organization my mother founded and ran was called 'The Fellowship of Service'. With my training, I was happy to help her although our remedies were largely cosmetic. Once a week we would gather in a hall in the town and, with a band of helpers, distribute clothes and food to the most needy cases. Local business people donated goods and money for the purpose. The cocoa commonly used by the natives was pure and unrefined, retaining the rich cocoa butter unlike the powdered form packaged for the European market. We handed out solid cones from which portions could be grated to make a thick and nourishing drink. The crowded hall became hot and stuffy after a while with the smell of unwashed bodies, and yaws and other unattractive tropical disorders made the weekly appointment quite an ordeal.

In the days of slave labour, sugar production had been the main industry and many ruined sugar mills were scattered around the island. Sugar was grown on some of the other islands and the rum derived from it made a popular drink, blended with lime or other ingredients and mixed with a 'swizzle stick'. Of the many estates scattered through the island, some were West-Indian owned, others in the charge of managers for European absentee landlords. The local peasants were of mixed race with African origins and land hunger was a constant factor. In this respect it was not unlike a period in Irish history.

At the heart of Grenada in an ancient crater was a deep dark lake known as the Grand Étang. There, in the dense tropical vegetation of trees and creepers, lived a troupe of monkeys that had been imported from Africa at one time and seldom wandered far. A young one was caught as a pet for me and lived in the mango tree in front of our house. He was an amusing creature but his pranks sometimes went too far. We didn't entertain much, but from time to time were obliged to give rather formal dinner-parties. The monkey would remain quietly at the top of his tree observing all that was going on in the dining-room, his bright mischievous eyes watching the best silver and dining service being arranged with great care. When all was finished and the servants had departed he would sneak in and seize cutlery, spoons or glasses, which he then secreted in the hollows of his arboreal home. Just before the company was expected frantic efforts would be made to induce him to return them, but to no avail; however, as the guests arrived in their finery they were pelted from the armoury in the mango tree. This antisocial behaviour was not likely to add to our popularity and so our little simian was returned to his lakeside playmates. Perhaps this had been the object of the performance all the time. He was not my only pet. I also kept a pair of armadillos, one of the few animals native to the country.

I was put in charge of the housekeeping and expected to give value for the time that I had spent studying the subject. The fat good-natured cook was more experienced than me after her years of working for Europeans with diverse tastes and, indeed, tempers. She did most of the shopping, going out to market every day with her basket on her head. Around the stalls she had time to gossip with other domestics from different houses. She bargained shrewdly for fruit, vegetables, fish and meat, and if she made a little on the side she had probably earned it. We ordered the main groceries from the local shops and they were delivered. The fruit and vegetables were much the same as in the Seychelles. Papaw or papaya was our special delight, eaten with sugar and a squeeze of lemon. If meat promised to be tough we wrapped it for a short time in the leaves of this same tree and the enzyme pepsin that they contained achieved miracles. We had to be careful not to do this for too long or it rendered the meat strong-tasting. The avocados, which were large and plump, we ate with Worcestershire sauce.

Neither the amiable cook nor I could do justice to our culinary skills as my mother had instructed that no highly spiced foods were to be served, believing they were not good for my father. My father was abstemious but he did like a drink at sundown as was the general custom. Again this was frowned on by mother for health reasons, and some people may have wondered whether the Chief Justice had a drink problem when they received secret notes from his wife before a visit asking people not to offer him a drink!

There was no actual colour bar in Grenada but long-term white residents whose families had lived there for several generations were very careful to preserve the purity of their European strain as far as possible. This was possible to do successfully if you had sufficient money to travel to the other islands and collect a mate with different blood lines, but for 'poor whites' it was not so easy.

In the days of transportation for political prisoners or, in many cases, for those convicted of what now seem quite petty crimes, many were sent to labour in the sugar plantations of the West Indies. This was a punishment worse than it would be today as medical science had not then got to grips with the problems of malaria and other tropical fevers. Even in their isolation these people tried to remain separate and not to marry into the black population.

In the seventeenth century many Irish people, so-called rebels, were exiled to Barbados and other islands. One came across such names as Killikelly, Cooney and Keane in the most unexpected places. In a steep valley between the capital Saint George's and Gouyave on the western side of Grenada was a settlement of whites whose forebears had been exiled by Cromwell. They had never married outside their community and often showed the results of inbreeding in their appearance. Although Grenada had good schools, education was not then compulsory and these people lived completely isolated lives, outcasts as far as the locals were concerned, and avoided by their fellow whites, if indeed they were aware of their existence.

The original inhabitants of Grenada had been Arawaks, more of the Red Indian race. When the French owned the island, before it was taken by the British in 1762, they harassed these noble people to such an extent that, like the Jews at Masada when the Romans approached, they thought death was preferable. They threw themselves over a high cliff into the sea at a place called to this day Sauteurs, from the French word for jump. Occasionally one met a survivor of these people, easily recognized by a reddish complexion and distinctive features.

Romance had not yet entered into my life and I had remained utterly indifferent to the opposite sex. This state of affairs was soon to change in the manner of a Victorian novel. The man who impinged on my emotions was a bright young Welshman who was Director of Education on the island and also headmaster of the boys' secondary school. I had met Martin from time to time at the Aquatic Club or in the houses of friends, but had never taken him seriously until it became obvious that he was showing an unusual amount of interest in me. My parents had inclined to the idea that they could regulate every aspect of my life. While they took a dim view of this rapidly developing situation they also considered that I was probably the latest infatuation of an easily infatuated nature. After all, there were few other girls on the island to choose from.

In the small British community resident in Grenada most people got to know about this frustrating courtship and, as well as being hugely entertained, also made it their business to invent various ways in which we could meet. They would arrange parties to which we were both invited and mischievously observe the annoyance of my parents when they heard about it. Their opposition accelerated the development of a serious love affair.

In 1934 Princess Marina of Greece married the Duke of Kent. It was naturally an important day and the ceremony was broadcast on radio. Few people in Grenada had receiving sets, but as a dinner guest at a local doctor's house on the night before the ceremony I was asked if I would like to come and listen in. The impetuous Welshman who was also a guest jumped up and offered to drive me there.

In the morning I got up much earlier than usual, crept out so as not to wake anybody and made my way up the hill to a little garden attached to Government House. Here a shelter looked over a wide distance. Never before had I seen a Caribbean sunrise. The spectacle was breathtaking. There down below was the tiny harbour and the expanse of dark sea. Then as the sun climbed it spread wide its golden mane along the horizon and lit up the water to a shining mauve, while gradually the little boats drew into the harbour returning from a night's fishing. My observations were interrupted by the toot of a motor horn and running down towards the road I saw the familiar, rather battered blue car with a large mongrel dog sitting in the back seat. Off we set and enjoyed the pomp of the wedding carried so far over the air. Then it was home again. As I walked up the drive I encountered my father shaving on the verandah, and the ensuing scene was rather stormy.

By Christmas-time strong action had been taken and no letters or telephone calls were allowed between us. A new element of intrigue was introduced. We had a maid called Caroline who acted as my messenger and Martin had a house servant who did the same. On Christmas morning I walked out of my bedroom at the far end of the bungalow and onto a verandah just opposite the servants' quarters. I heard a low whistle and a figure darted out and handed me a parcel. I hastily snatched it up and just had time to take it to my room before my mother appeared saying she thought she had heard someone. I avoided explanations, but I feared to use the bottle of expensive perfume in case questions should be asked. There was little chance of us ever exchanging a word and my Welshman's friends advised him to give up his pursuit as the situation was obviously impossible and his work was suffering but, as the saying goes, 'Love will find a way.'

Life, meanwhile, went on much as usual. I played tennis at a club attended chiefly by West Indians. They were much better than me and probably found me a great trial, but they were too polite to indicate so. I ran a children's club for locals as I had done in England, and enjoyed the contacts that I made. Sometimes I went with friends for short trips to neighbouring islands. One day a terrific thunderstorm forced us to land and seek shelter in a fisherman's hut. Grenada then considered itself out of the hurricane zone, but some years after we left, the island was hit very seriously and most of the extensive spice groves were destroyed. For a long time afterwards the islanders had to depend on bananas as a cash crop.

Occasionally judges from neighbouring islands would come for a Court of Appeal and we had to entertain. At other times my father might have to don the ominous black cap and pronounce sentence of death. This happened very seldom but my father, a kind-hearted man, hated it and on the day of an execution we almost went into mourning, not going out and behaving even more soberly than usual.

Sometimes we gave a dance, ostensibly for me but my father took over. We had a gramophone with a few battered records, and he loved old favourites such as 'Gold and Silver' and 'The Blue Danube'. He was not at all pleased when a young guest whom he had previously rather admired turned off Strauss and put on something more to her liking. My mother, who stuck firmly to the tenets of her upbringing, never danced. In the bishop's household such frivolities had been frowned upon. Life might have been happier had she been able to bend a little.

The time then came for us to leave Grenada. My father was retiring and returning to his 'homelands' as an African might describe it. As it was winter we spent a while in Tobago off the island of Trinidad. We chugged there in a small steamer and put up in a secluded hotel. I shall always remember it as the island of the hibiscus, which bloomed everywhere along the hedges and driveways. Tobago was then relatively 'undeveloped' as the all too ominous phrase puts it. The empty white beaches were virginal in their purity, and the water was limpid and pollution-free. It was before the invention of plastics, which have been such a blessing in some ways but such a curse to the environment, and no residue of this material lay around. The people of the island liked to believe that Tobago was the original site of Robinson Crusoe's sojourn.

Afterwards we returned to Trinidad and travelled by ship back to Europe. On leaving Grenada I had not been allowed to communicate in any way with my ardent but necessarily secret suitor. For the first time in my life my emotions were aroused and I pined and couldn't eat. As a family we all sat at the captain's table, a privilege expected by my father. People remarked upon my lack of appetite, and soon aspects of my story became known, the passengers without exception taking my side. They included Sir Ernest and Lady Simon, a learned but jolly professor who was writing a book about the West Indies, a retired naval commander, and a much younger artist. Most were people who would normally have hob-nobbed with my parents rather than with me, and the situation became distinctly Gilbertian. A spirit of dare-devilment seized me and I embarked on an innocent flirtation with the artist, which relieved the boredom of the voyage for our fellow travellers as they devised ways of encouraging it and circumventing parental interference. My mother would rush up on deck for the post-prandial siesta to place her deck-chair firmly beside mine, only to find Michael and I already planted side by side, with a row of other passengers acting as support in their own chairs. Or else she would be directed all over the ship looking for me while I was on the bridge with Michael and possibly the captain. Games of 'sardines' were orga-nized where no one knew where anyone else was. Now that I have brought up my own family I feel considerable sympathy for my mother, but the 'permissive age' had not then been heard of. There was always a limit beyond which flirtation would not be likely to go. Most shipboard relationships vanished when normal life on dry land was resumed – 'Ships that passed in the night'.

I had spent so long slumming in London in preparation for the final year of study as a social worker, I naturally thought that on returning to Albion's shores I would be allowed to take up my diploma course, and Lady Simon, who had considerable influence, promised to help. My parents had never taken my aspirations seriously, and it was a shock to find that they had no intention of letting me have the money to continue my training at the London School of Economics. The LSE had left-wing leanings and the idea of my going there was anathema to my family. I had no money and was quite helpless. At this point I rebelled. I saw myself frustrated in a love affair and denied the possibility of completing a training I was more than half-way through. I was to go back to Ireland and live the life of a dutiful daughter. I refused, and such small allowances as I was receiving stopped. I was now over twenty-one and when we arrived in London I decided to go my own way. What was I to do? Should I try what was then considered a very dubious calling and become an artist's model, as suggested to me by Michael? What alternative was there?

My godmother Molly Bothamley came to the rescue. She took me in at the missionary hostel and found me a number of different occupations which paid for my keep.

I landed one interesting temporary job that lasted a fortnight. It was the Jubilee Year of King George V, and Queen Mary and he were touring districts of London in an open coach. In those days philanthropic settlements throughout the poorer areas of London engaged in various forms of social work. One, called The Lady Margaret Hall Settlement after the Oxford women's college of that name, wanted extra help over the Jubilee period. The royal couple were to pass in front of us and we were feverishly engaged in putting up bunting, flags, etc. The great day arrived, warm and sunny, and most members of the Centre, especially the children, were gathered in front of the entrance backed up by the staff. The King appeared rather solid and solemn, and Queen Mary, wearing the usual toque, smiled at the flag-waving crowd and nudged her tired consort as they passed us. They both turned and gave the royal wave, and with that the function was over and my job, which had also included joining in the general work of the Centre, ended.

I was unwell at this time as I had picked up a tenacious parasite in the tropics which took a while to eradicate. This was finally done and it brought me into contact with a Doctor Gordon, who had rooms in Harley Street and also lived there. He took a fancy to me and asked me to work for him. This solved my problems for the time being and I remained with him for about eighteen months.

Doctor Gordon belonged to the old school of specialists and had an imposing presence. He always wore a frock-coat and striped trousers, dyed his hair, which was beginning to turn grey, and carried himself well. I remember one occasion when he came into the consulting room in the morning, immaculately dressed, to preen himself before the mirror and then, noticing a blob of dye on the end of his nose, vanished upstairs with a look of horror. He used the old-fashioned wood stethoscope, but was by no means behind the times in the treatment he administered to his patients. He called himself a diagnostician and believed that the whole mechanism of the body should be studied before making a diagnosis for any specific ailment. He employed his own son as a full-time bacteriologist in a laboratory elsewhere. Every patient, on his or her first visit, was supplied with several containers for specimens, the analysis of which governed his treatment. Sometimes he had specific serums made, and he also favoured the use of the gold treatment, popular at the time for TB and other complaints. I was employed as his assistant nurse and chaperon-cum-secretary. I was untrained but assisted a fully qualified nursing sister who administered the many prescribed injections. She was Scottish and rather striking-looking, but was inclined to resent me.

Dr Gordon had been married and his wife became rather odd, so he said, after being bitten by a dog when their last child was on the way. The resultant daughter was, when I eventually met her, a woman of about thirty who was what would now be termed mildly mentally

handicapped. She had a sly, rather difficult character, but
was intelligent enough to sit downstairs answering the
telephone and making appointments. The doctor was a
lonely man in ways as he never spoke to his son, who
avoided him when he came to the house every day to
collect the specimens and deliver his reports. Instead he
fell back on the company of his rather wanting daughter.

It was at first agreed that I should live in the house
and keep Miss Gordon company. She soon became
jealous and prevailed upon her father to make other
arrangements, so I went to live at a YWCA and travelled
daily to Harley Street. Before this the doctor and his
daughter decided to take holidays in Scotland and left me
in charge. I had few duties and had the place to myself
except for the two maids whom I was supposed to
supervise. At twenty-two years old it was quite beyond
me to control these sisters, one of whom was about
twice my age. They made the most of their liberty and
enjoyed themselves both in the daytime and during the
night-watches. Not surprisingly, a few months later they
both gave notice as the younger one was complaining of
nausea.

Doctor Gordon was unique in Harley Street in that he
used the whole house rather than letting any of it to
other doctors. Every morning at half past nine I would
walk from Bedford Square to Harley Street, arrive at the
red-brick house and proceed down the steps to the basement door which led to the small sitting-room I shared
with the nursing sister. Here I donned the white coat
and nurse's cap and climbed two flights of stairs to the
twin consulting rooms. It was customary then for a doctor
to have some other female present, preferably a nurse,
when he was examining a woman patient. This was one
of my duties and I supervised the various lamp and short-
wave treatments that were part of the routine. In this
way I was given some instruction.

It was a society practice with a mixture of the eccentric
and the simple and genuine people who had tremendous

faith in the doctor. There were lonely spinsters who appeared hale and hearty but who came regularly for electric treatment and, one felt, were in search more of male attention than a cure for their ills. One such lady was sure of the doctor's personal attention with no nurse present. Once when by mistake I walked in as he was solicitously bending over the couch, I was told in no uncertain terms to get lost. Then there were the TB patients in those sad days when so many people died of that disease, coming for the gold treatment as a last hope.

One noble lord of somewhat mixed reputation would turn up whenever he was staying at the Cavalry Club. He had a habit of appearing out of the cubicle, which was set aside for changing and supplied with a dressing-gown, stark naked, leaving behind him his pure silk underwear embroidered with the family crest. After one visit he presented the doctor with a profusely illustrated book. The unappreciative recipient was so shocked by its apparently pornographic contents that he rushed into the room where I was working and demanded that I take it back at once to the club. It was November and the fog was so thick that I couldn't see my hand in front of me. I found myself wandering about almost completely lost, seeking an address I had never been to before. It was a strange errand to send a young girl upon to a man with a bad reputation with women, and in such weather. Our titled friend had two regular mistresses. They were not particularly glamorous and of more or less uncertain age. The twain were naturally never allowed to meet but each visited the doctor with complaints against the other for having a debilitating effect on her lover.

It was the time of Oswald Mosley, and some of the patients were greatly influenced by his ideas. One couple from the country was full of fascist enthusiasm. They were breeders of silver foxes and were unique among our visitors, as it was on behalf of these animals that they came. They persuaded the doctor to use his laboratory to discover exactly why the animals were not thriving. He

discovered that the trouble was a nasty tenacious parasite
known as whipworm, and that the owners suffered from
this problem too.

It is extraordinary to contemplate that all I received
was £3 5s a week, and yet with that I paid for a private
room, breakfast and dinner at night in the hostel, a light
lunch every working day, and had money over to buy a
few clothes in the January sales.

At this period Martin returned from Grenada, on pro-
longed leave to study for his Diploma in Education, and
rang me out of the blue. Unhappily it was when I had
been left in charge while Doctor Gordon and his daughter
were away, and on the day that they were expected to
return. As a rule, I was at liberty to go and come as I
pleased, but on this occasion I was expected to await
them in the house. I decided, in my excitement, that I
would take a chance and probably be back well before
the couple returned. I arrived back to find Miss Gordon
busily muttering into her father's ear. The situation was
tricky and I rang up my faithful godmother Miss Bothamley, who came over and explained all. As a result the
dear old doctor fell in love with her and could be heard
talking to himself as he walked up and down, 'If only
things had been different.'

My parents' attitude was now beginning to soften,
though they still considered it frightfully 'infra dig' for a
girl with the name of de Vere to be working as I was.
My father had grown tired of domesticity and the role of
lord of the manor and wanted to build a house in Cyprus
and plant an orange orchard there. He appeared from
time to time in London while making plans, and would
ring up during the day asking me to come for a drive in
his new car. He found it impossible to understand why
my job was anything more than a passing whim that
could be abandoned during working hours.

He said that having inherited his home he never had
the pleasure of planning one himself, and this he sought
to do. He finally did build his Cyprus house, while my

mother remained in Ireland and I pursued my independent way with Doctor Gordon, but he scarcely lived for long enough to enjoy it, taking seriously ill and returning home to die a few months later in 1936. I regret that we never established a mature relationship in my older years when we might have come to understand each other more clearly.

SIX

Two For Company: The Gold Coast and Ireland

SHORTLY AFTER Martin's return on leave and our ill-timed meeting in August, we became engaged. My parents no longer opposed the idea. London was fun then, even if one had little money. In the side-streets little cafés proliferated where it was possible to get a satisfying lunch for under half a crown, while one and six bought a good seat in the cinema where we would go in the evenings, supping adequately afterwards on herring roe on toast. The underground was inexpensive and its farther reaches made for many an interesting trip. Martin stayed in a cheap hotel in Russell Square where he discovered that the clientele was mixed: from the sadly ageing film extra made up to the eyebrows and waiting for the call, which often came, to the visiting prostitute and, to his surprise, to the nurse who worked with me at Doctor Gordon's – in the evenings she blossomed out, made several passes at Martin, and was given to collapsing on the stairs in her night-gown asking to be carried back to bed.

On the 14th of April 1936 we were married at Christ Church, Woburn Square. It was a quiet wedding as my father was very ill, and only a few friends and relatives were invited, among them Doctor Gordon who unfortunately didn't turn up. He always set great store by his appearance. A slight accident had befallen him in which he had bruised his face and, being absurdly vain, he was not prepared to appear in public.

For our short honeymoon we went to Ireland, bringing our own car. At Holyhead we saw a *Daily Sketch* picture of our wedding pinned inside one of the offices, and outside our cabin porthole a sailor walked the deck singing, at the top of his voice, a song with the rather staggering refrain, 'She charges a tanner, she charges a bob, it all depends on the size of your knob.'

As we motored along country roads we reached the Galtee mountains which were still covered in snow, though the sun was warm. Then we crested the hill and the proud stretch of the familiar woods of Curragh Chase lay before us. The trees were just taking on the tender green of springtime, birds were busy in the nesting sites and bluebells beneath the tall plane trees in the pleasure-ground swept towards banks of primroses beside the paths. There we roamed the grounds endlessly, so different from the solitary wanderings of my childhood, making a wish on the wishing-seat, our movements no doubt closely and secretly watched by Eggie and the maid from the scullery window of the house.

This window was covered with a heavy wire mesh which made it impossible to see in although it was quite easy to see out. I had often stood at that window myself with some member of the staff, watching some unsuspecting couple. 'Are they linking?' Eggie would call, anxious to discover the exact nature of the relationship. The Green Room held no ghostly fears for me now that I had a companion in the large double bed, and the log fire which was lit only for the ill or special guests cast comfortable shadows.

We returned to London and cheap lodgings near Regent's Park, where at night the roaring of the lions could be distinctly heard more often than in Kenya. *A Midsummer Night's Dream* was put on in the park, and to this day I can remember the effect of the late summer light, the trees and the far-off summer lightning playing across the sky.

As soon as Martin had passed his examination we headed back to the West Indies and sunny Grenada. While Martin had been away a number of changes had taken place. The call of 'The West Indies for the West Indians' had become more strident. A Trinidadian was now headmaster of the boys' school and Martin had only his duties as school inspector. The voyage out had been the usual pleasant interlude marred only by the fact that the next generation was already knocking at the door. I suffered badly from seasickness to which I had previously been immune.

The few months that we were to spend in Grenada were happy enough although Martin worried about how long any of the posts now held by Europeans would so remain. We had dinner parties in the houses of friends and one at Government House where I was treated in the manner traditional for a bride of not a year and placed on the right of the Governor, taking precedence over other women of greater importance than myself. The waistband of my best evening dress was let out and I prayed sincerely that sickness would not overtake me.

Our maid, called Misère, was an elderly wizened little woman who had been rescued as an infant from the island of Saint Lucia when her parents and many others perished in an eruption. We befriended a wonderful old Catholic priest called Father Gates, a reclusive and saintly man who lived in a primitive little house way up in the country. He was an exquisite artist and painted most of the flowers indigenous to the island. After his death the paintings were sent to a gallery in the United States of America.

Far along an isolated road in a distant part of the island a Church of England parson looked after his little flock. His wife was very pretty and young. She pined for lack of congenial company with only a small infant to talk to, and every now and then would attend a dance in Saint George's complete with infant. A senior government official, who was normally rather reserved and had been badly wounded in the First World War, fell for her and she for him. The husband wisely decided to apply for a post in England, and for several days after the boat sailed his wife's admirer went around with a bunch of forget-me-nots in his buttonhole.

I was looking forward to having my baby and bringing it up in that balmy clime, but that was not to be. About three months before it was due Martin was told that he had been transferred to West Africa's Gold Coast where he had served for a time before. Packing up those wedding presents that we had taken out in hope, and looking more like a barrel every day, I accompanied my husband back to England on a voyage that was a nightmare as I was seasick all the time. The influence of Adolf Hitler, gaining strength in Germany, was evident on that Hamburg-Amerika liner *Caribia*. The Christmas Eve party was preceded by the 'Horst Wessel Song' and the raised arms of most of the crew. The captain regularly gave a modified form of the Hitler salute when he appeared in the dining saloon in the morning. None of us was fully aware of the momentum that lay behind the Nazi movement.

It was a peaceful scene which met us when we arrived in Plymouth on Christmas Day 1936. The buildings ringing the harbour were wrapped in the quiet of the festive season. Coming in we had passed three small white-sailed yachts and repeated to ourselves the well-known carol beginning 'I saw three ships come sailing by on Christmas Day in the morning,' and we spent that night in the port which shortly was to become the target of many a German bomber.

Our ten-pound son was born on the 2nd of March, 1937, in Cardiff, his father's home town. Martin had left three weeks beforehand for his appointment in Accra on the Gold Coast. I found it hard that the Colonial Office would not allow him to stay at home over the short period to see his first child. In many ways the birth of a child at that stage had a profound effect on the pattern of our marriage. In those days marriage and family life for anyone who found himself appointed to 'the white man's grave' was very frustrating and it was almost impossible for a wife to fulfil adequately her twin vocation of spouse and mother.

That summer the baby and I found ourselves at Curragh Chase where my mother, wearing heavy widow's weeds, was living alone. It was like returning to the days of my childhood, except that now I was a mother myself. It was wonderful having the run of that large house again but I was kept in my place and not encouraged to take over any responsibilities other than those connected with my child. In these days of central heating and electricity it is hard to realize that even the simple task of bathing an infant in a stone-cold bedroom took care and preparation, and in spite of the great advantages of country air and extra help, colds and bronchitis were a constant worry. Now antibiotics are close at hand but in those days a cold could lead to pneumonia and often to death.

After six months the imploring letters from Accra became too much for me and I made arrangements to go out to the Gold Coast for a visit. I left the baby with my mother who kindly offered to care for him with the help of a nursemaid. To ask any mother to be parted from the child that she has been breast-feeding and watching develop goes against the most fundamental instincts, but nevertheless I took off, this time by the *Elder Dempster* from Liverpool. The journey lasted three weeks so there was plenty of time to get to know fellow passengers, many of them young wives who had also left children behind. The sea was rough when we arrived at Accra and we were hoisted overboard onto the waiting dinghy by what was called the 'Mammy Chair' – a seat lifted over the side by a crane.

My stay of nine months on the Gold Coast was one of the happiest periods of my life. I did not mind the heat and with a comfortable bungalow, a cook and a houseboy, it was a time of relaxation. The Gold Coast then was a very prosperous and well-run colony. No European government official was allowed to have any business or mining interest in the country, nor were Europeans allowed to own land, so there was never any accusation of graft. Martin as a school inspector spent much of his time travelling over the district and I went with him. Atta, our delightful and faithful houseboy, packed up the necessary equipment, including that important item, the chamber-pot, and carried it to the car on his head. We put up at small isolated rest-houses, and when the heat allowed I enjoyed exploring the countryside. I was never so happy as when I was in the heart of the bush with those strange, inimitable bird-calls coming from the top of the tall trees and every movement among the leaves intimating the presence of some exciting and unusual creature.

After three months we moved to Kumasi, the capital of Ashanti, where the large and dominant tribe of Ashanti was ruled over by the tribal chief known as The Asantehene. Here I was able to develop my interests. I had been asked to collect African butterflies for the British Museum, so when my husband was attending to his duties I wandered far afield, net in hand. I never felt any fear of the burgeoning life all around me as I netted the exotic giant butterflies floating from tropical flowers or feasting on moist dung left by some animal. It was an interesting hobby with all the elements of the chase and the Museum was pleased with the results. In later years I developed a strong reverence for life and could not bear to destroy any living thing in such a way.

Any Africans I met were friendly and welcoming and although at times I forgot the hour and a worried Atta would come looking for me, it was only for fear that I had lost my way and not concern for my safety from the locals.

During the remainder of my time there we got to know a Mr Kidman-Cox, a delightful member of the Agricultural Department, with whom I fell platonically in love in the restrained way habitual to me. He fired my enthusiasm on the subject of orchids and I became an addict. We considered starting to collect specimens of local varieties, some of which had not been identified before and were sought after by Kew Gardens in London. The idea was that we should collect some for them and that they should then supply us with some of the more exotic types to set up an orchid business in the Gold Coast. It is difficult to convey the excitement I felt among the trailing vines and epiphytes hanging from the giant trees, suddenly spying a green rosette or cascade of

an orchid species, with a delicate spray of bloom hanging 103
from its centre. It was all the better when, after carrying
it home with pride and consulting the botanical guide, I
discovered that it was indeed an as yet unnamed species.
Gathering the plant was the most difficult part. Sometimes
I had to mark the spot and call upon the faithful Atta the
next day to 'shin up' the tree and collect it for me, taking
care that it did not harbour any noxious insects or
snakes. I did not feel that there was any harm in this
collection as it was for scientific purposes. There was no
difficulty in preserving the orchids in hanging baskets
once I got them home.

My husband got local leave while I was with him and
we took a trip in a vessel travelling along the West
African coast. In Nigeria we stopped for a short time at
what was then the small port of Calabar. Weaver birds
were building their ingenious nests in the bamboos
beside the wharf and small children paddled their minia-
ture canoes across the smooth waters of the bay. This
was before oil brought financial gain but ecological loss
to the spot. I had been raised on the story of the pioneer
missionary Mary Slessor; twin children were considered
to be unlucky and she had rescued many of them from
certain death. She became so much loved and such an
expert on local customs that she was given administrative
powers by the British colonial government. I stood in
reverence at the grave of the 'White Queen'.

We continued our journey and came to French
Togoland, under Gallic rule since the Treaty of Versailles.
It had previously belonged to Germany which had
administered it fairly, if strictly. The Germans had built
themselves a home from home there, in spite of the
climate, with a bandstand in every small town and streets
lined with mango trees. The French and the Africans were
still in constant fear that the Germans would reappear.

We had as a fellow passenger on the ship an intrepid
old lady called Miss Twemlow. She carried on a flirtation
with the chief officer and the chief steward, convinced

that they were fascinated by her charms. She came with us on several shore trips and was both inexhaustible and fearless. On one occasion, walking along a dirt-track in the heat of the day, we came to a river in full flood with only an insecure rope bridge across it. I refused to cross having always had a fear of heights. It did not deter Miss Twemlow, however, and from the swaying centre she called out scornfully, 'You have been brought up too soft!' On our return journey we passed the Spanish-held island of Fernando Po, where we were forbidden to land in those days of the Spanish Civil War. With our field-glasses we could see troops drilling and the white-robed figures of the Moors that Franco deployed against his own people, a strange move when one considers Spain's victory over the Moors in the days of Ferdinand and Isabella.

Back on the Gold Coast we often travelled to places where other white people had died a few years previously of yellow fever or sleeping sickness. Just before I had gone out it became possible to be inoculated against yellow fever, which was a great relief. I was once attacked by a swarm of the fever-carrying tiger mosquitoes with their yellow-striped bodies. The tsetse fly, a kind of horse-fly, carried sleeping sickness, and was very common near game or cattle. It attacked anything moving such as a swinging arm or leg. A story went the rounds of a young recruit who was travelling out to West Africa in those days. The old-timers amused themselves at the unfortunate man's expense, telling him gruesome tales of fevers and deaths. When he arrived at Accra a fellow passenger asked him to dinner for the following night. When he arrived he was met at the door by an African houseboy who told him, 'Master no live.' 'Good God,' he exclaimed, 'dead already!' and fled from the house, not learning until the next day that 'Master no live' was merely pidgin English for 'Master not at home.'

The climate and the constant anti-malarial doses of quinine told on me and after nine months I again boarded the *Elder Dempster* and returned to England and thence to Ireland. There was no trouble about importing the orchids as regulations were not so stringent then. I just placed the box underneath the bunk in my cabin and was able to deliver them in person to the curator of the Botanic Gardens in Glasnevin, Dublin. That was the end of 'Operation Orchid' for within two years the war came. I never went back to the Gold Coast and Kidman-Cox of the Agricultural Department joined the Forces. There was, therefore, no point in arranging for the plants to be sent to Kew Gardens.

When I returned to Curragh I found my son David thriving, if rather too fat, and I began to appreciate the trouble my mother had taken in being responsible for him throughout the winter. It was not very long before Martin himself came on leave. Like everyone else we rejoiced at the time when Chamberlain brought us the news of 'Peace in our time'. People later never fully appreciated what a respite he provided. He tried to achieve peace, and how we longed for it, grasping at the smallest straw. In the end that respite helped an unprepared England to mobilize her resources. Neville Chamberlain was related by marriage to the de Veres through Annie Cole, his wife, who spoke of how broken-hearted Neville was at the way public opinion turned against him.

We rented a little house in Rustington on the south coast of England for the period of the leave and before Martin was due to return to Africa I was once more pregnant. Hostilities became more and more likely, and training Spitfires wove through the sky as people gathered in knots to discuss the future. There seemed no point in remaining in England, especially on the south coast, so I returned to my kind and long-suffering mother at Curragh Chase. There everything was peaceable as usual and life went on much the same in a country sworn to neutrality. It was a glorious summer and golden autumn, and my mother was occupied in putting up a memorial cross to my father on a high spot in the woods. It meant a great deal to her and it is still there. On August the 14th our second son Patrick was born in the beautiful Octagon Room. It was very many years since the house had known the fruitful labour of birth. It had been said that the house had a curse on it and a male heir would never be born, but then Patrick was not the heir. Overhead the planet Mars hung every night in an almost unprecedented fiery red glow – Mars the God of War – and in September hostilities began. For the rest of the war years I lived sometimes at Curragh Chase and sometimes in Greystones. Martin braved the submarine threat and came home on leave from time to time. He was very lucky. His friend was lost on a ship he himself would have travelled on had his passport been in order.

While living in Greystones in December 1941 I got the news that Curragh Chase had been burnt to the ground in an accidental fire. It was a few days before Christmas and my mother and two maids were alerted by the library bell ringing downstairs. There were rumours of careless guests and cigarette-ends in waste-paper baskets, but no one was quite sure of the cause. The water pressure was poor and the fire-engine late, there being no telephone. Very little was saved and the house took its memories and its secrets with it. I often felt that Eggie the housekeeper suffered most from the loss. Someone remarked, 'Now the curse has gone,' and the lady whom some visitors claimed to have seen in the Green Room was seen gliding beside the lake, ousted at last from her place of haunting.

Our third son, Aubrey, was born in Dublin in March 1944. After the war in Europe ended and shortly before the dropping of the atom bomb, Martin developed typhoid fever in the Gold Coast and was invalided home for good. Thus began a new period in our lives. We began to explore other parts of Ireland and other ways of making a living. Vere, our fourth son, was born in June

1950 in Derry, when we were running the Royal School, Raphoe, in Donegal, and finally Grace, our only girl, arrived in July 1955 while we were living in Queensboro, where Martin taught Latin at Drogheda Grammar School.

We went almost every summer to Curragh Chase where my mother, like Eggie, lived in one of the cottages, devoting herself to the welfare of the older retainers on the estate even after the property had been bought by the Forestry and Land Commission in 1957. She was heart-broken to see the wholesale and indiscriminate tree-cutting. The beautiful lime avenue was destroyed for no particular purpose, and the banshee of the power-saw wailed unceasingly. I think that this hastened her sudden death in 1959.

In the fullness of time Curragh Chase has blossomed once again. The Forestry Department has become more enlightened, much planting has taken place, and Curragh Chase is now one of the most popular Forest Parks in the country. History has returned to the people the land taken from them in earlier days, but enriched by the care and development of generations of loving and attentive private owners.

For me, however, it is the unkempt secret places of Curragh Chase that I miss: the corner of the wood where the blue-jays called; the mossy cairn in the Deer Park where the best ferns and the purple hellebore grew; the quiet petrifying stream which met the lake at a point where freshwater mussels hid in the mud; and the uncut stretch of lawn where orchids and other wild flowers blossomed. On a quiet evening, when visitors have left, it is still the same shade-haunted spot, with the sound of the water birds coming from over the lake scarcely interrupting the immense stillness.

APPENDIX

James Lees-Milne on Curragh Chase

Sir, I send the accompanying photograph [omitted] as a record of Curragh Chase, near Adare, Co. Limerick, which was burned to the ground on Christmas Eve.

Curragh Chase was for centuries the home of the de Vere family through the marriage in 1573 of a Henry Hunt with Jane Vere, a younger daughter of Aubrey de Vere, the second son of John, Earl of Oxford. This branch of the family (for the Hunts only assumed the name of de Vere two and a half centuries after this union) have always considered themselves the rightful claimants to this illustrious earldom. Curragh, until its recent tragic end, had been most fortunate in the devoted care and attention it received over a number of years from Mrs Stephen de Vere, the widow of the last of the de Veres.

Curragh Chase was a late eighteenth-century or early nineteenth-century classical building incorporating far older portions, in one of the most remote and romantic settings conceivable. I believe there are no houses, other than a lodge or two, nearer than four miles away. 'Bosom'd high in tufted trees,' the house was surrounded by dense and luxuriant woods, with, in the distance, the clear outlines of purple mountains. Below the terrace wind the silent reeded banks of a lake from whose very waters you would not be surprised to learn that the mystic arm of the Lady of the Lake once grasped Excalibur. No wonder Curragh was a sanctuary for poets of the Romantic school. Sir Aubrey de Vere (1788–1846) was well enough known in his day as the author of *Julian the Apostate*, *The Duke of Mercia*, and of *Mary Tudor*, whereas his younger son, Aubrey (1814–1902) – who was born, lived all his long life and died at Curragh – was one of our greater Catholic poets. He was the close friend of Patmore and Hopkins and of Tennyson – who frequently visited Curragh, where he wrote that absurd poem, 'Clara Lady Vere de Vere' – and most of the Victorian poets and artists.

The poet's library – where Aubrey de Vere wrote so much and that 'Sonnet to Sorrow' in the *Oxford Book of English Verse*, beginning, 'Count each affliction, whether light or grave, God's messenger sent down to thee.' – was left exactly as it had been during his lifetime. His books, his beautiful writing table made of Curragh woods, his chair, his portrait, all helped to retain the wonderfully undisturbed flavour of peace and meditation that enveloped the whole of Curragh. Among countless literary and historical treasures, now presumably destroyed, was the small gold and enamel crucifix (containing a piece of the True Cross) which Charles II, on his deathbed, handed to Father Huddleston, who had saved the king's life after Worcester. In course of time, this precious relic was given to Aubrey de Vere.

Is it, I have been lately wondering, more sacrilegious, sentimental or perhaps selfish of me, who have known Curragh, to derive a sense almost of satisfaction in the particular brand of fate that has befallen this truly enchanted place? For, surely, a lingering, mouldering end to a great house whose beauty is so intimate and indefinable as was Curragh's, is far, far sadder.

(from *Country Life*, 3 April 1942)

. . . I was first taken to Curragh Chase in 1938, and perhaps a second time in 1939, by a friend of mine, Richard Stewart-Jones, long since dead. He was very devoted to Mrs de Vere and extremely taken with the romance and isolation of Curragh. I remember it as a house that seemed to have escaped time . . . the tranquillity of the place was almost deafening.

(from a letter to the publisher, 21 November 1989)